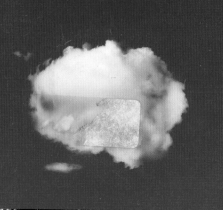

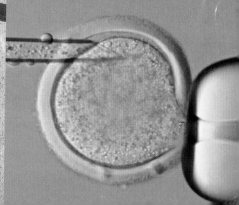

The
Circle

Kala Bailey

The Circle

HOW THE POWER OF A SINGLE WISH CAN CHANGE YOUR LIFE

LAURA DAY

ATRIA PAPERBACK

NEW YORK   LONDON   TORONTO   SYDNEY

ATRIA PAPERBACK
A Division of Simon & Schuster, Inc.
1230 Avenue of the Americas
New York, NY 10020

Copyright © 2001 by Laura Day
Originally published in 2001 by the Penguin Group

First Atria paperback edition March 2009

ATRIA PAPERBACK and colophon are trademarks of Simon & Schuster, Inc.

For information about special discounts for bulk purchases,
please contact Simon & Schuster Special Sales at
1-800-456-6798 or business@simonandschuster.com.

Designed by Deborah Kerner and Nancy Singer

Manufactured in the United States of America

10   9   8   7   6   5   4   3   2   1

ISBN-13: 978-1-4391-1821-4
ISBN-10:   1-4391-1821-3

CONTENTS

PREFACE

I made my opening presentation for *The Circle* on September 10, 2001, at a local bookstore near the World Trade Center; my neighborhood, my neighbors, and readers all gathered to welcome this book into the world. I didn't know why then but we all felt unsettled that evening. The next day, I watched a plane fly into the World Trade Center as I emerged from the subway after dropping off my nine-year-old at school. What was to follow changed me forever. Our small neighborhood and our world community came together in the most extraordinary union of mutual caring and support. The air was thick with dust and smoke but in the two weeks that followed, I was also surrounded by a Circle of hands in need of the gifts I had to offer and hands offering their generosity to me.

My book *The Circle*, which had a press tour planned, was left in the hands of the reader; and there it flourished. As I tended to my son and our friends and then re-entered our evacuated neighborhood, our Circle strengthened. Readers began Circles of their own. People at my local bookstore came out of the woodwork to help. Edward Ash-Milby made sure the book was always on the shelves; and Caroline Hughes scheduled a once-a-month free

Circle for the community, which I led and which continues to thrive at our new Tribeca neighborhood store. Miwa Messer scheduled events wherever they were needed countrywide, and readers invited me to join The Circles they had created. Bill Barbanes snuck past barriers to feed my cat and answer reader mail, and he created a website that gave *The Circle*'s readers a forum for sharing intuition and healing with others.

In the following years, *The Circle*'s readership grew and with this growth came many suggestions and improvements by its readers. I acquired my agent, friend, and fierce advocate, Jennifer Rudolph Walsh; and my visionary new publisher, Atria Books, with Judith Curr at the helm and Johanna Castillo, my editor, making sure everything was perfect.

Most of all I have been blessed with you, a Circle, a world community, of intuitives and healers with the courage to be teachers who share *The Circle* with others.

I am blessed beyond words with the guidance of others. Every day I personally answer every email, which often contain gifts of readings, healings, and blessings for my family and me. My tissues accompany me each morning as I read stories of people reborn through their own efforts incorporated from *The Circle*. I have learned to pray with new commitment as I send healing each morning to every person who joins me. This reminds me that hope is rational, miracles are routine, and brotherhood and sisterhood are the true power of being human.

The Circle was a gift to me. It flew from my fingers, to guide me to safety. In my darkest moment, before I wrote my first book, the simple truths that form the basis of *The Circle* led me to successfully write *Practical Intuition* and to re-enter the world in a powerful, joyful, and authentic way.

I have created so many "wishes come true" with *The Circle* in my own life. My wish for the past few years has been "family." True to *The Circle*, family has been provided to me in more forms, with more beauty and richness than I could ever have anticipated. You are now part of my New Reality. Welcome to my family and thank you for making my life so much more beautiful by your presence.

Included in this new edition is the Workbook that I've personally used to keep my intuition, my energy, and my choices directed toward creating my dreams and the dreams of those I love. I hope that it serves you in the same way that it has served me. I recommend that you take and use The Circle Workbook on your own journey.

I now offer this new edition of *The Circle* to you—in truth, it was always yours.

Please share your journey by contacting me at Healingday@aol.com or by visiting www.practicalintuition.com.

The
Circle

PROLOGUE

Welcome to The Circle.

Though it has been known by many names in esoteric practices, The Circle is a discipline that has been used for thousands of years and is not in conflict with any religious or spiritual beliefs. If it helps, you can reframe my words about The Circle in terms of your own belief system.

One of the most profound traits that distinguishes you from other animals is your ability to imagine things that do not yet exist; your ability to envision future possibilities and to choose among them; in short, your ability to create.

This is a course, then, in human being.

Most of you have lost touch with your innate human ability to create. You are creating your life right now, each and every aspect, the bad as well as the good. Your ability to manifest your dreams is directly related to your ability to consciously connect with all of your inner resources and tap into the infinite resources of the Universe. You are about to learn that you have far more inner resources than you ever realized. In fact, you'll learn that you have all the resources of the Universe at your disposal. You must simply know how to ask.

If creation is as simple as that—and it isn't much more complicated—why don't you realize it in your everyday life? Before I consciously entered The Circle, I had visited it countless times without awareness. You have, too.

Have you ever had one of those delicious moments when everything in your life just seemed to "click"? If so, you were within the energy of The Circle. Have you ever had a dear wish come true? If so, you were in The Circle, which allowed your inner readiness to join in harmony with outside events. Have you ever experienced a moment of despair, when "out of the blue" someone or something entered your life to turn your situation completely around for the better? If so, you were in The Circle.

The Circle is an energetic state of being that allows you to connect with yourself, with others, and with the transformative powers of the Universe. In The Circle, what you perceive, what you conceive, and what you create are one—and you are at one with the infinite energy and possibility of creation.

You can view The Circle as a metaphor. Imagine the place where everything you are connects as one energy with everything around you. Think of yourself and of your abilities as the inside this Circle. Its circumference is where you make contact with the outside world: others, events, your environment, the present, the future.

When you change any element of these energies, you change them all. By allowing your circumference to become part of a larger Circle of energy, you become a powerful force for change.

You are an active part of the machinery that creates the world and its events. For every internal part of you—each thought, wish, fear, experience—there is an external correlate. When you change the message in your being, in your very atoms, this change affects every person and every event on the planet—and sets in motion the unlimited powers of the Universe. Miracles begin to happen for you. You begin to create miracles for others. The place where all of this happens is The Circle.

There is no magic to miracles. We can encourage their occurrence by using our will to create a resonance that attracts sympathetic energies. Miracles reflect the interconnectedness of seemingly unrelated individuals and events. Miracles present us with unmistakable glimpses of The Circle.

For those who live outside The Circle, life is a struggle. For those within, life is limitless possibility. I invite you to see life not as a struggle, but as a source of inspiration. In The Circle, all things are possible.

If you've had a difficult life—and we all have had our struggles—this

Create anything

statement may sound incredible; yet before you finish reading this book, you will experience this truth firsthand. You will learn to take everything in your life—yes, even your losses, your wounds, your hunger, your anger, and your grief—and use it as creative energy to shape the world you want.

Give over your wishes and worries to the energy of The Circle. In The Circle, all our needs are supported. Our vulnerabilities transform into abilities. Our fear and vigilance turn into insightfulness and sensitivity. Our anger becomes the energy of action and healing creation.

In The Circle, you will discover that you have everything you need. You are enough.

This is not a "how to" book but rather a "what is" book. The Circle simply is. It is there to help you. Or not. The choice is yours.

You can consciously create anything you want. You can be anything you want, once you master yourself and your abilities to project your energy and intent to the world around you. When you are aware of this place, you can create and transform anything. Once you have consciously entered The Circle with your whole self—mind, body, and spirit—you have access to all the knowledge and power of the Universe.

Right now, as you read these words, The Circle is working for you or against you. No one is sure just how The Circle works. Did you fall off the Earth today? Of course not. Neither has anyone else. Long before we understood how gravity worked—and even our greatest scientists have merely described and quantified its operation—gravity operated in our lives.

You do not have to trust The Circle. You do not have to accept the human gift of conscious creation on faith. The alchemy of The Circle will transform you. Simply make a wish and follow The Circle. It will lead you to belief.

I invite you to join me in a journey to a special place where you realize your dreams. I have divided your journey into three sections of three elements each. Though mastery of all nine elements is your goal, you may find some sections of the journey easier than others.

Initiation introduces the tools and readies you for the next stage. Apprenticeship gives you practice in applying the tools in everyday life. Mastery helps you apply the tools to help others and to teach others how to use the tools. In the final stage, the student becomes the teacher.

You can read this book however you choose. You can read it once through before delving deeply into the mysteries of each element, or you can dip into whichever one seems most relevant to your current situation. Allow your intuition to guide you.

You may want to start your Circle Workbook—located in the back of the book. Doing so will be daily confirmation of the power of your intuition, your healing, and your ability to manifest miracles. The information in your Circle Workbook will be enlightening to you for years to come. If you do The Circle in a group or with a friend, you will want to include in your Workbook their intuitions concerning you. And in The Circle Workbook you will find a blank page where you can put pictures, poems, objects, or illustrations that help you gain a deeper understanding of The Circle and yourself.

By the end of this book, you will be an intuitive, a healer, and the conscious creator of your own reality. You will experience your innate gifts of alchemy. You will be able to turn the elements of human being into the materials of creation. You will know that you have achieved mastery by choosing one thing in your life that you want to change and changing it.

When you have mastered the elements of The Circle, you will have mastered life. You will finally realize that you are an alchemist of all energy, of all being, and that you can transform anything. When you have mastered the gifts of human being, you master The Circle. When you master The Circle, you are at one with the Universe.

Allow me now to be your guide. When you have completed The Circle, you will guide others.

As you begin your journey within The Circle, you may think that you are traveling alone, but that is not the case. I join you within the energy of The Circle. We are in The Circle together. You will soon discover yourself surrounded by people, energy, and events that support you and your conscious creations.

You are not alone. You are home.

To enter The Circle, you need only to make a wish. We will begin this process by discovering your heart's deepest desire. In your initiation, you discover your one true wish and put it into the language of The Circle.

Initiation

The First Element
I N T E N T I O N A L I T Y

The "practical" people of the world are quick to dismiss "wishful thinking," and yet the process of creating anything begins with a wish. Wishing focuses your internal resources—intellect, intuition, unconscious drives, and physical and emotional energy—on any creation you choose.

Wishing is the active, engaged sister of fantasy. Your imagination ignites desire and then hunger to initiate the process of change. Without the motivation of desire, without hunger, you would achieve nothing since you would want for nothing. Your hunger drives you in search of nourishment, just as a plant turns toward the sun for more light and deepens its roots for more water.

You experience hunger in many ways. Desire is hunger. Envy is hunger. Loneliness is hunger. Everyone is hungry. Artists are hungry. Students are hungry. Scientists are hungry. Entrepreneurs are hungry. Visionaries are hungry. Humanitarians are hungry. All of us are hungry. Hunger drives you to expand what and who you are.

Yet you often distrust your desires. If you fear you cannot satisfy them, it seems safer to repress your hunger. You have made hunger the enemy, but hunger is life. When you repress, judge, or deny hunger, you deny life.

Do not fear your hungers. They are neither good nor bad. Use hunger as fuel. Use hunger as energy. Guide your hunger. Focus your hunger. Use

Journal

your hunger for growth. If you do not consciously direct your hunger, your hunger will use you and those around you.

Go ahead—dream of what you want. Allow yourself to wish. Allow yourself to feel your hunger. In The Circle, nobody endures hunger.

When you make a wish, you direct the energy of The Circle. You give yourself—and the Universe—a positive focus, a path for energy to travel.

The use of will is the magic wand of human being. Yet very few of us use our wills effectively. Your will organizes and mobilizes all the other energies inside of you and around you into an irresistible force. Your ability to make a choice and stick to it—your will—is your most powerful inner resource.

Since this is your first conscious journey in The Circle, you must focus all of your being on one, single wish.

Take your time now in selecting your wish. Ask youself many questions. Let your mind run free. Draw up a long list, then narrow it down.

What single change in your life would give you the most joy? What single change would bring you the most relief? What is your biggest concern? What issue do you spend most of your emotional energy on? What lack is the source of your greatest sorrow? What is the one thing that you most envy in others? If you knew you couldn't fail—as if a genie would grant it—what would you wish for?

Keep in mind that a wish need not be "reasonable" or "rational" or "deserved." Nor is a wish a "should" or a "must" or a "would have." Your wish now should be the thing you ache for, your soul's deepest need.

Lots of Money!

You may have many desires, so it may not be easy to decide on just one. For now, though, you must choose just one wish to create as you master the nine elements of The Circle. The Circle is always there to travel again with another wish, but during your initiation, when you are just learning the ways of The Circle, you should focus on a single wish. Otherwise, you may dilute the energy being built up around your primary goal.

As you reach one goal, you will form new ones, and The Circle will help you with all of the mini goals that arise during the day. Doing one thing well and effectively will positively impact all areas of your life. Also, there is no possibility that you will select the "wrong" goal. Your needs and desires will become clarified within The Circle. If you choose a wish at odds with what you truly want, that wish will evolve to serve the wholeness of your being and your life.

So what do you wish for right now? Make your wish. One, single wish. Together we will begin to bring your wish to life. You can also write it in your Workbook.

In the past, you may have wished for many things that you did not receive. There is an alchemy of wishing. It's time you learned to wish within The Circle. To do so, you must express your wish in a way The Circle will respond to. *The language of The Circle is the present tense.*

When someone experiences an event as happening in the future, it does not yet exist for that person. And if something does not yet exist, it is not possible for that person to experience it and change it.

In The Circle, the acts of wishing and receiving are simultaneous; there is no distinction between past, present, and future. The future occurs now. So in The Circle, there is not "I want," but rather "I have." Phrase your wish as if it has already happened.

If you focus on "I want," you direct your inner resources to reinforce *wanting* rather than *having*. If you focus on "I have," "I am," "I feel," or "I embrace," your inner resources will find opportunities for this to be true.

So instead of saying, "I wish I would fall in love," within The Circle you say, "I am in love." Instead of saying, "I wish I weren't struggling financially," you say, "I am earning all the money I want, doing something I love."

Once you wish within The Circle, we call your wish your New Reality because it is already happening, right now.

It is also important to phrase your wish positively, in terms of what you want, rather than negatively, in terms of what you might be trying to avoid. When you wish in the negative, you focus your attention and energy on the very thing you don't want, which directs your unconscious to reinforce it.

Instead of focusing on what is not happening at work, say, focus on creating recognition and success. In doing so, you direct your inner resources to notice opportunities to achieve your goals that you would otherwise have overlooked.

Instead of, "I wish I weren't sick," you say, "I am healthy and full of energy." Instead of saying, "I wish I weren't alone," you say, "I am involved in a loving, committed relationship." Remember always to phrase your wish as if it were already fulfilled.

If your wish is to be heard within The Circle, then, it should be specific, positive, passionate, and present. Wish for one thing at a time, know precisely what you want—and embrace that wish with all your heart and soul as if it has already come to pass. By doing so, you will unleash amazing energies.

State your wish out loud. Now embrace it. You are creating yourself and the world anew.

THE FIRST
ELEMENT IS
INTENTIONALITY

The gift of intentionality is
CONSCIOUS CREATION

In the circle below or in your Circle Workbook, write your wish in the positive and in present tense. This is what you have chosen to create. When you place your wish in The Circle and in your reality with conscious intentionality, all the gifts of your human being—as well as its connection to all that is—co-create this reality with you.

Your wish is now your New Reality.

The Second Element

EMBODIMENT

Vision Board

Now that you have made your wish, it is crucial that you experience it and act as if it has already occurred. To embody your wish is to embrace it today, right now, even though it may not have completely manifested itself to you.

Since you become what you embody, you are fostering a self-fulfilling prophecy. Sometimes you must count your chickens before they hatch, or they may not hatch at all.

You will be creating an energetic framework of what you must draw toward you from the outside world to realize your New Reality in a manner that enhances all parts of your life. This framework gives your inner resources powerful guidance in noticing and attracting the right people, events, and experiences into your life.

It is time to take your New Reality from the abstract. Many people have difficulty imagining things in a full and detailed way. But if you cannot imagine and create something internally, you will find it difficult to create it in the world.

If you are writing in your Circle Workbook, you may want to record your wish, your New Reality. Write or draw a detailed representation of your New Reality. Be as descriptive as you can, as if you were experiencing your life today with all of the detail that surrounds you. Do not be concerned if you cannot immediately envision every single aspect of your New Reality.

Throughout the coming days and weeks, both your intuition and the events that you will be creating in your life will give you new details to add to your description. You may want to rewrite your wish at the end of each chapter as you master the elements of The Circle and as your wish becomes more of a reality in your life.

Now that you have described your wish, take a moment to embody it fully with all your senses. The senses are a universal language of being. Our senses are mechanisms for receiving information. Our brain takes this raw data and uses it to draw conclusions and create understanding. Even the most abstract, cerebral concepts of physics and mathematics are based on what we experience through our five senses.

Don't simply visualize your New Reality. Speak your New Reality aloud. Experience it with all of your senses. Breathe and fill every atom of your being with your New Reality. What does it smell like? What sounds surround it? What does it feel like?

Now look around you. Observe how your life has changed now that you are living your dream. Where are you within the New Reality that you have created? How do you think? How do you look? Who is with you? How do others look to you?

This process of embodying, of fully experiencing, what you are creating should be repeated as often as possible. You can do so as a ritual at set times each day or whenever the inspiration moves you. Each time you do, your wish becomes a truer part of you and of your life, and you are that much closer to your New Reality.

At first it may be difficult to embody your New Reality. There may be a place within you that cannot fully feel it, see it, or experience your wish. Learning to embody fully takes time and practice. The more fully you can embody your wish in the present, the more quickly it becomes real in fact.

If, for whatever reason, you simply cannot embody your New Reality— pretend. When you were a toddler you pretended that you could read, and lo, now you can. Sometimes we must take baby steps to our New Reality.

One way to embody your New Reality is through "reality tales." A reality tale is a story or collection of stories about how your New Reality was created (remember, it already exists).

A reality tale is intended only as one possible scenario, not a prediction. For example, let's say a person's New Reality is to earn her living through her art. Her reality tale might go something like this:

I gave some of my pottery, my favorite hobby, away as gifts. A woman at a friend's dinner party saw a piece that I had made. As it turns out, this person ran the design depart-

ment for a chain of stores. She asked for my phone number and called me for an interview to design a line of pottery for her stores. Within a few months, I received other offers. I felt secure enough to quit my job at the accounting firm. This step had the added benefit of leaving me the time and energy to go to the gym regularly. After a short time, I was in great shape and more relaxed than ever. At the gym, I met a wonderful man on the treadmill next to mine. We were married later that year and moved into a great apartment that had studio space so that I could work at home.

Your reality tale can be as short or as long as you like. You can write a new one each day in your Workbook as a ritual. Think, sing, write as many as you are inspired to do. Reality tales prime your intellect, intuition, and subconscious mind to notice opportunities that will help you realize your wish. They put your master plan into The Circle while allowing you to focus your energy—and the energy of others and the Universe—on your New Reality.

Your New Reality may materialize in a completely different way from that envisioned in your reality tales, but you will be surprised how often they are prophetic.

It is important to embody your wish because everything you think, everything you feel, and everything you do are reflected in the world. Our whole Universe is composed of atoms. These atoms all work together. When even a single atom changes, it affects its neighbors, which affect theirs, rippling out and ultimately affecting all of the other atoms in the Universe.

You, too, are composed of atoms. The atoms that compose you are constantly being affected by all of the other atoms of the Universe. Your atoms, in turn, are constantly affecting every other atom in the Universe. When the information in your atoms changes, this change affects every other atom of your being, of the world, of the people around you and the people at a distance, and of events past, present, and future.

In short, when you change yourself, you change the people and events around you. By embodying your wish as if it has already occurred, you reprogram not only yourself but also the Universe.

Each of us is both a transmitter and a receiver. When we meet a new person, a series of unconscious questions almost instantaneously runs through our minds. For example: Who is this person? What is his history? What does he want? What can he offer?

The messages that this person is sending out are picked up by both our conscious and unconscious minds, which provide us with the answers to these questions within moments of making contact.

The people we encounter, even our own friends and family, ask many of the same questions of us. For better or worse, our signals become embodied in others and are reflected in their ideas and actions.

You are sending out signals all the time. These messages are blueprints for other people in the world to find you, react to you, and connect with you in a certain way. What you are is reflected in every person, action, and event around you. Everything you think and feel is experienced and reacted to by the environment and by the people around you. To a great extent, you are what you believe you are—and the world responds accordingly.

Think of a tuning fork that creates sympathetic vibrations in others. Quite literally, whatever message you embody will resonate in others.

In this moment, everyone around you, whether in the same room or miles away, is receiving and responding to your thoughts and feelings, just as you are responding to theirs. This mutual process occurs even when you and they are separated by space or time.

Neither you nor they may be aware of this process. The only evidence that this subliminal communication is indeed taking place is in the reactions in your environment. You may think, "I wish Jane would call," when, out of the blue, Jane calls. You may feel angry with your husband just when he walks into the room—surprise—acting defensively. You may feel positive about your professional abilities, just before job offers synchronistically come rolling in. When you are in love you attract love. Just as you accept a job offer, another always seems to follow.

You continually send out the same messages and attract the same people and experiences toward you with little variation. Like many of your abilities, these messages tend to be shaped and patterned by your early experiences. All thought, action, and energy have a pattern. If you are sending out a conflicting pattern, people respond to the confusion accordingly, and events may clash with us.

It is important, then, that you become aware of the message that you are sending others—and the Universe. Is it a clear message, one that reflects your New Reality? Consciously assemble a message from all the feelings surrounding your wish, as if you were delivering this message directly in all of your interactions. Remember that you are delivering this message to the people and events in the world even when you are unaware of it, even when you are separated by space and time.

When your inner resources are organized, your conscious direction of energy is stronger than the fragmented energy of others around you. When you are the most decisive pulse of energy in a situation, you guide the energy and motivation of the world around you.

When you fully embody your New Reality, the very pulse of who you are changes, and you reprogram the messages you are sending out. The answers that come from your very being—your voice, your posture, your gestures, your unconscious facial expressions—will convey a clear message of the New Reality you are creating. In turn, you receive different responses from others and your environment, those now in keeping with what you want to create as opposed to what you were living unconsciously in the past.

⊗ This needs to be
Congruent w/
your Other Mind's Eye

The following Circle meditation will help you internalize, embody, and then project your wish. You can record yourself reading it—feel free to modify it as your intuition suggests—so that you can listen to it with your full attention.

You will now enter The Circle with all of your being. Notice, for a moment, the energy within you. Allow yourself to be fully aware of the atoms of which you are made. As you breathe, become each atom within you. The subtle atoms of thought. The electric atoms of feeling. The magnetic atoms of intuition. The living atoms of physical being. Become the perception of all these atoms moving, relating, and affecting one another.

Feel, see, experience yourself as these atoms. Allow yourself to become aware of the patterns of flow among all of your atoms. Notice their movement, their dance, and the patterns and programs that they contain. Billions of atoms are working together within your being, each one changing, moving, and shifting from one moment to the next.

Each atom knows exactly what to do. Each atom's inner program directs its being and its interactions with every other atom around it. The order of your atoms' movements is patterned by you, your ancestors, and nature—from the habits and beliefs absorbed and modified by each generation right down to your very DNA.

In The Circle, you are creating new patterns, new programs of your own conscious choosing. Your being will support your New Reality, as your New Reality will support your being.

Use your breath to diffuse the illusion of your solid body. Now notice the spaces between the atoms of your being. Allow your breath to fill these spaces. From these spaces, your breath fills every atom of your being. From your breath, you ready yourself to enter a New Reality of your own creation.

As your energy becomes programmed with the energy of your New Reality, notice how your energy affects the energy of the air around you. Notice that every atom of air now moves and responds to your New Reality, as if your New Reality were part of the air's internal program. As you breathe and allow your New Reality to be embodied with you by the air around you, allow the energy of your New Reality to radiate outward until you can feel it embodied by every being, every structure, and every event in the Universe.

Notice the energy of the Universe and the energy of your New Reality as one energy. Embody, along with every atom of the Universe, the New Reality that embodies all. Know that you will consciously embody your New Reality in every moment of every day as the world embodies it around you.

Again, become aware of all of the atoms that move together to make you. Allow each of these atoms to embody your New Reality. As you embody your New Reality with every atom of your being, extend your awareness to the atoms of the air around you. As you breathe in, allow yourself to become aware of how these atoms make contact with the surface of your skin, with the inside of your nose and your lungs. When these atoms come in contact with you, they absorb the elements of your New Reality, and they change.

As you breathe out, notice how this contact expands with your exhalation. Your thoughts, your breath, the charge of your emotions, and your being all expand. As you expand the breadth of your being, you expand your awareness of, and your effect on, the world around you.

Allow yourself to experience your wish come true, your New Reality, with all of your senses. What does life look like in your New Reality? What does it smell like, taste like, sound like, feel like? How do you think, feel, respond, now that your New Reality is your life?

Your wish has come true. You are now your wish, your New Reality, with all of your senses. You have programmed every atom of your being, even the spaces between your atoms, with your New Reality. With every breath you take, allow your wish to become more and more real.

Allow all your senses to perceive it. As you experience your New Reality, allow yourself to feel your connection, your oneness, with every other atom of the Universe. Allow yourself to feel every other atom responding to your change and embodying your New Reality with you.

Your New Reality is now being co-created by every atom, every being, every event, and every energy in the Universe. Know that as I co-create your New Reality with you, you are co-creating my New Reality with me.

THE SECOND ELEMENT IS EMBODIMENT

The gift of embodiment is
AWARENESS

When you embody anything, you use all of your senses and abilities to create full awareness. Whatever you are aware of, you can change, master, and fully enjoy.

The Circle meditation, on page 24, will bring you, your New Reality, and the surrounding Universe together in one energetic state of creation. You can reread The Circle meditation each time you want to consciously enter The Circle. After a while, you will be able to enter The Circle simply by being aware of the energetic state that you learned through practicing the meditation. For now, use the meditation to begin the exercise below.

Enter The Circle.

Embody your New Reality with all of your senses, including the thoughts and memories your senses create. Experience your embodiment with each of your senses, one by one, then allow them to dance with one another to fully create and experience your New Reality.

Bring the energy of embodiment to all areas of your being. Dance your New Reality, dress it, draw it, sing it, walk to it, breathe with it, share it with others. Bring the pulse and rhythm of your New Reality into every gesture and interaction.

Become more aware of your New Reality, and act and interact with its guidance to create reality tales with the thoughts and situations you encounter. Begin now by creating a reality tale that begins in this moment and takes you to your New Reality. You can record your reality tale in your Circle Workbook.

The Third Element

RITUAL

Intentionality, the first element, underscored the importance of replacing unconscious living with conscious choice. With the second element of embodiment, you continued the process by living your wish. The third element, ritual, furthers this process by replacing many of your unconscious habits that have no connection to your current wish with conscious rituals that reflect it.

In a sense, rituals are an external equivalent of embodiment. Just as embodying imprints your wish in your conscious and unconscious minds as well as in the energy of the Universe around you, rituals imprint your wish in your environment, everyday actions, and outer life. Rituals give form and shape to the events that you are creating now and empower them with sacredness.

A ritual is any act performed in a ceremonial or intentional way, usually on special occasions or on a recurring basis. Rituals need not be religious in nature. We can use them to acknowledge the profound importance of anything.

Rituals are distinguished from habits, the soulless reflexes that allow us so easily to sleepwalk through our lives. Rituals are important because we invest them with meaning. The difference between rituals and habits—

between the sacred and the mundane—is the meaning with which we empower things. The same glass of wine can accompany dinner—or communion.

Sadly, most people never truly break their habits, no matter how hard they try. Year after year, they slip into the same patterns of thoughts, feelings, and behaviors. Sometimes, one pattern is behind what they see as several unrelated incidents, and they never realize that they have been repeating the same script since childhood.

You each have habitual patterns of thinking, feeling, and behaving that have been practiced for so long and have become so integrated into your life that you are no longer conscious of them. Indeed, much of your life is lived unconsciously through a patterned set of habits, some dating from before you were able to speak. I have seen adults, in times of stress, make sucking motions with their mouths, as they must have made as suckling babies seeking comfort from their mothers.

Modern times have become so complex and are lived at such a fast pace that you give over great chunks of your waking life to your unconscious: how you wake up, how you eat, how you get to work, even how you relate to others. Habits allow you to function on automatic pilot, saving you from the need to think about situations before you respond, saving time and freeing up your conscious mind to attend to more important matters.

To be sure, some of your habits serve you well. Others, however, serve only to reinforce the difficult patterns in your life. Indeed, your old reality has probably become embedded within your habitual patterns. Yet situations change, you change, and what formerly was a useful habit can now be getting in your way—without your awareness.

When we live too much through our unconscious patterns, we create unconscious lives. Your habits may contain forgotten meanings associated with them, meanings that keep you trapped in your old reality. Your waking-up habits may be infused with the anxiety or limitations of your childhood home. Your habits for greeting people may have developed from an old need to keep others at a distance.

When you embody your New Reality within The Circle, you will begin to discover habits and patterns you didn't know you had. You may notice for the first time, say, that when an attractive person of the opposite sex greets you, you look away and avoid contact. Or you may notice that when something good happens in your life, you reflexively seek out something bad to happen next. Awareness is the first step in change.

In The Circle, all habits and familiar patterns that do not support your New Reality will begin to seem uncomfortable. Rituals, which are intentional models of what you want to create, will help you overcome the inertia of your old habits and routines that are hindering your New Reality. Sometimes all it takes is a single, simple change to catalyze a cascade of further changes in every aspect of your life. Small changes, such as going to work by a new route or eating lunch at a new restaurant—or at a new time, or not eating lunch at all—are often enough to shift the entire "axis" of your life. If you continue to consciously re-create your rituals, you will manifest lasting change.

In The Circle, you create rituals that repattern your inner and outer selves in preparation for your New Reality. In practicing these rituals—imparting sacredness to your changes and using the energy of conscious repetition—you dissolve old patterns or behaviors that hinder the realization of your New Reality, salvage what is still useful, and reaffirm in every movement the creation of something new. Years of negative reinforcement are reversed within the collective energy of The Circle.

Rituals help you realize your New Reality in many ways. Sometimes doubts arise, and we have difficulty embodying our New Reality in our minds. At such times rituals hold us up; sometimes it is easier to act as if our New Reality has come to pass than to believe it. Rituals help us maintain our focus and intention at all times. In a sense, rituals are spiritual training wheels, though ones we should never discard.

Rituals elicit profound mental and emotional responses from us, and they gain force the more they are practiced. By performing rituals over and over, we train ourselves to summon these positive responses on demand.

By "etching" your goal into your subconscious mind, rituals create order in the midst of confusion. Our rituals create a pattern, a map not just for us but for the Universe to follow in the creation of our New Reality. Rituals re-educate our unconscious patterns of energy in a directed way. Your New Reality will happen as quickly or as slowly as you are able to accept it. Old patterns of reality are often hidden from us. In these patterns lurk the vestiges of our old reality.

In creating your various rituals, you may want to adopt a special place at which to conduct them. We call such a place your "sacred space." A sacred space reflects your inner connection to the Universe. It is a place where you worship the sacredness of your being, supported by the sacredness of The Circle. It is an external representation of The Circle.

Having a sacred space allows your inner resources to repattern and recharge. It is your own external cue that you are safe and at one with all that is good. In a sacred space, you can easily use your inner resources in the ritual of creation. It can be a place of meditation, or a place where you perform rituals surrounding your New Reality. It can be filled with elements and symbols of the New Reality that you are creating in your life now. You can invite others to join you there.

Most likely, you have already created a sacred space without realizing it. It might be a special couch, a preferred room at home, or your favorite garden bench. It is important here, as with all the elements of The Circle, that you do things as consciously as possible.

You can create a sacred space anywhere by bringing sacred intent into a location. Many cultures have altars, which people feel allow them the ability to connect to a greater or universal power. Your sacred space can also be your favorite chair, your favorite place in a park, anywhere your surroundings connect you to your own inner peace. Combining comfort with the images, sounds, and scents of the ideas and things that support you creates a sacred space. You can carry your sacred space with you wherever you go by imagining it with your inner eye. Your sacred space may not look sacred to anyone else. As with the rituals you adopt, your sacred space has a special meaning because you consciously endow it with such.

Now, in this moment, allow your intuition to lead your senses to the sacred space within you. Allow yourself to experience the colors, sounds, smells, scenes, and people of your sacred space. What is the language of your sacred space? Is it song, writing, art, scent, nature? What higher power or higher parts of your own being do you want in your sacred space with you? When you know the qualities of your sacred space, you can re-create it everywhere.

Sometimes you unconsciously cling to your old reality. You can use rituals to mark the passing of your old life as well as to usher in your new. Only by adopting new rituals of thought, action, behavior, and expectation can these old patterns be reworked into a New Reality. By replacing old patterns with new rituals, you create not only a New Reality but also a healed self.

The Circle will lead you to transform your rituals and allow them to transform your life. You become your rituals. What do you want them to bring you?

You can create rituals anywhere at any time that support your New

Reality. Rituals can be effective whether they last a few seconds or a few hours. What matters is that each ritual be a beautiful gesture that speaks to your spirit and soul. A ritual can even be embodied in a melody, drawing, or other symbol, so that its mere presence instantly triggers a positive internal state. Indeed, symbols speak to our unconscious in a different and often deeper way than do spoken or written words.

You can create a ritual around anything, from the way you get up in the morning to the way you greet strangers to the way you prepare your food. Set an extra place at the dinner table for the partner you expect to enter your life. Light candles when you bathe and allow the water to "dissolve" your extra weight as the candles "melt" it. Cover a notebook with drawings of your New Reality or create a collage of your New Reality and hang it in front of your bed. Make your bathroom a temple of rejuvenation and your bedroom a temple of love.

Each of the other elements can be ritualized, too. One Circle student cleverly designed a ritual around her reality tales. She made a ritual of writing down in her calendar future events that would occur on the way to her New Reality. Use rituals to mark changes in your life, whether positive or negative.

Celebrate the successes and victories. Acknowledge and mourn the losses and allow the energy of disappointment to become the energy of faith and transformation. And always honor the journey.

The gift of ritual is

SACREDNESS

Ritual empowers the act of creation. A ritual begins with intent. You decide what you want to create—joy, love, a new home, a closer relationship, a healthy body—and you create its pattern through ritual.

Here is a simple format for a ritual:

Gather things that represent for you what the ritual is intended to create. This could include objects, artwork, prayers, candles, herbs, food, anything that represents your creation.

Enter the energy of The Circle. You can experience The Circle meditation on page 24 to connect with The Circle.

Consciously call upon any higher power that you believe in to join you in The Circle. If you have no such beliefs, you can call upon the power of your own subconscious to aid you. You may want to begin with a prayer from your religion or create a prayer that intends the highest good of all concerned.

Create something that embodies your intent. If you want to attract love, you could sculpt you and your lover out of clay. If you want to create physical healing, you could hold a glass of tea in your hands and drink it, knowing that as the fluid enters you it heals you. You could draw a picture of your New Reality and carry it with you throughout the day.

End with a prayer or affirmation that leaves your creation within the energy of The Circle. Rituals can be integrated into daily activities. When you sit at the breakfast table with your family, raise your morning juice glasses to make a toast to a great day. Hug your child or spouse with joyful intention. Well-wishing is one of the most powerful blessings we can give.

My Circle Book
- My reality tale has to describe
how my wish impacts every
area of my life in detail.
" Chapters" for each, Pictures
(vision board) for each.

- Use of Active Imagination +
One's own Mind's Eye to
identify any part of me that
could resist the New Reality.

- New Reality at level of
Identity - My writing the
check for 200.ᵒᵒ tonite
to Jim for groceries was my
first concrete action
to come from that new
Reality ⇒ I have all
the money + resources
I need now!!

Apprenticeship

I did this process when I
~~did~~ decided to take Mom home
hospice

- House was cleaned
- Water pipe dug on a Saturday!
- Bed to house + O2
- Moving people (ripped me off)
- Mom's cousins daughter was
  her hospice nurse
  TV hooked up
> "saw" a hospital bed propped
up in the living room
  w/ pink sheets on it. I have
  those sheets.

- Lorraine in Session.

My head + my heart
were congruent. All
of me was in my
intent.

The Fourth Element
SYNCHRONICITY

By making a wish and embodying it within The Circle, you have sent a clear signal to the Universe. The process of change within The Circle has begun. Your wish is already coming true. You don't need to "do" anything. All the energy of the Universe is now focused on creating your New Reality with you.

Know this: External events will begin to align themselves around your New Reality. When you wish within The Circle, the entire Universe and everything in it—every being, every event, every energy, and every moment—create your New Reality with you. You will find that the world and the people in it conspire to help your wish come true. The strangers you see on the street are co-creating your New Reality with you, whether they want to or not. You are co-creating their realities with them, whether you know it or not. Right now, as you read these words, you are helping to materialize my wish for me, and I am helping to materialize yours.

As often happens when you enter The Circle, signs that your New Reality is on its way have already begun to appear in your life. You may not always be aware of their full significance immediately, but in time you will. Seemingly out of the blue, wonderful opportunities will be presented to you at a rapid pace, opportunities that often seem like nothing more than remarkable coincidences.

You notice these opportunities because, by wishing within The Circle, you have put your intellect, your intuition, and your unconscious on notice to gather any and all information and other resources you need to create your New Reality. Louis Pasteur, the brilliant French chemist, once said, "In the fields of observation, chance favors the prepared mind." He was offering advice to young scientists that is relevant to us. Although good fortune often plays a role in scientific discovery, it is only when someone has prepared himself that he will be ready to notice the tiny chance events that help solve problems.

Pasteur was right, but I believe that these "chance" events, the ones that come unexpectedly to our aid, are not accidents.

Though you haven't yet fully realized their significance to your New Reality, seemingly inexplicable "coincidences" are going to play a dramatic role in your life.

Did you ever acquire a new skill or a piece of information—only to encounter suddenly a wonderful opportunity to use it? Did you ever meet someone at a party and have a great time and then encounter this person everywhere? Did you ever need cash to meet some unexpected emergency when, out of the blue, you receive a refund check from the IRS for past overpayments years ago?

These are synchronicities. Such coincidences will happen all the time now that you have entered The Circle. This process of attracting synchronicities is not magic. It is a gift of human being.

A synchronicity is an especially meaningful coincidence that defies conventional or scientific explanations. We can also call synchronicities "meaningful coincidences" or "serendipities." The simpler phrase is "good luck."

So now that you have wished within The Circle, be aware that pieces of your New Reality are already being presented all around you. The trick is, these pieces may not be in a form you expected!

Again, the usefulness of these synchronicities may not become apparent until days or weeks or even months later. Nonetheless, never lose sight that once you have entered The Circle, all these events will conspire to move in the direction of your New Reality.

This is true even when the chain of events begins on a disappointing note. For example, you may have wished for a job promotion, when instead you get fired. A week later, while going to the library to research potential jobs, you bump into an old friend you haven't heard from in years. Surprisingly, he tells you that there's a job opening at his company for someone with exactly your qualifications, at an even higher salary and responsibility level than the promotion you'd originally hoped for.

Or perhaps you wished for a passionate and loving relationship with your partner, only to discover that he had recently been unfaithful. If you stay within The Circle, you can turn even this trauma into a healing transition. Either the two of you can now resolve the issues between you or you know it is time to leave the relationship. Either way, the synchronicity—

however painful a revelation it may have been—has moved you that much closer to a profound love relationship, either with this person or another.

Take a moment now to become more aware of the events that take place on this journey to your New Reality. Use your Circle Workbook to record the synchronicities you encounter each day. Acknowledging the good luck that you create in your life allows you to use your inner resources more confidently and powerfully.

Once you enter The Circle, all events are meaningful passages to your New Reality. In other words, now that you are within The Circle, everything that happens is good luck.

THE FOURTH
ELEMENT IS
SYNCHRONICITY

The gift of synchronicity is
EFFECTIVENESS

Consciously enter The Circle. You may want to re-experience the meditation on page 24.

Feel the pulse, the rhythm, the pattern of your New Reality.

As you breathe, notice everything around you responding to this rhythm, dancing the dance of your New Reality. You may want to get up and move, breathe, and gesture to the rhythm and notice how the room, the air, the light respond to your pulse.

As you go about the day's activities, allow this rhythm, the rhythm of your New Reality, to pulse through every moment, word, interaction, and gesture. Notice how the events around you begin to respond to the pulse of your New Reality.

Use your Circle Workbook to record the synchronicities that you encounter: the obstacles that you become aware of and the people and events that come into your life "out of the blue" to help you create your New Reality. Effectiveness is the result when you work with the element of synchronicity.

The Fifth Element
MAKING SPACE

When novices embrace their wishes, they invariably do so without considering the changes their New Realities will require of them. It is as if they view their dreams as things simply to add to their current lives, like a new car. Nothing could be further from the truth.

To accommodate your New Reality, you will need to make myriad changes, major as well as minor, often in areas far beyond those immediately surrounding your wish.

Your New Reality needs space. When you focus on creating something new, the Universe requires that you grow, and space is a pre-condition for growth. You will also have to make both internal and external adjustments in your life. The changes you will need to make may be difficult. You may notice that you need to let go of certain situations and people in your life. Remember that you must make changes in all aspects of your life, not just the one area you're focusing on.

Think of a couple awaiting the arrival of a beloved newborn, with all the changes their New Reality will demand. They have certainly considered the obvious purchases they must make: a crib, a stroller, diapers, and assorted paraphernalia. Perhaps they have anticipated other adjustments, such as more irregular sleeping hours and less sleeping time. But have they considered how parenthood will affect their respective leisure hours or job performance, their interactions with each other as well as those with their friends?

You have now chosen your path and brought it into The Circle. Every moment of your life now presents you with the opportunity to live your New Reality. Everything is transforming around you and within you, including your perceptions and reactions.

Look around you at the changes that have already begun in your life. Though you may not understand these changes, and some may not be easy, embrace the process. Allow yourself to yield to your own inner transformation. Open your hand and let go of things that you have held on to out of habit for years, or even a lifetime. Stay within The Circle and allow its energy to carry you through the moments of transition.

When you made a choice—when you consciously entered The Circle with your wish—you committed your energy to a specific goal.

Now when you embody that New Reality before it is actualized, you create a blueprint for both yourself and the Universe to channel whatever resources are needed for your creation.

Though it may not be fully apparent yet, the process that you have begun is already affecting you in new ways. As you travel The Circle, you will find that change in your outer life and the world reflects change in your inner self. As you change, the world changes around you, facilitating further inner changes. You and your environment work in partnership to create your New Reality.

Embodying your New Reality activates the dynamic chemistry of change within you. Just as you have begun to notice synchronicities in your life, you will notice changes within yourself as well.

By consciously entering The Circle with your wish, you began the process of integrating a new pattern of being in readiness for your wish. The old you would not fit into your New Reality.

Your physical being will undergo changes. Anything in your appearance, movements, habits, and use of your physical resources that supports your New Reality will become compelling to you. You will physically become the person who can support your New Reality. However, the most important changes, of course, will occur within.

Not all of these changes will be easy to adjust to, though you will notice that all of them are moving you closer to the realization of your wish.

As you embrace your New Reality, you may find yourself eating, sleeping, thinking, and engaging life in a new way. You may find that you reconnect with people from your past to resolve old misunderstandings. Intuition may give your intellect a healing perspective on the past. Even your dreams may heal old wounds.

You are clearing your inner field to make room for creation. As old situations and patterns are released, their energy and wisdom are available to create something new, transforming your life and your being. The energy you spent hiding is now free to draw security and safety into your life. You can free yourself from the patterns that you made when your parents divorced or when you opened your heart to your first love and were injured. Transform the energy of these outdated patterns into the fiber of your New Reality.

In addition to these internal and external changes, your thinking and prioritizing will undergo changes; you will acquire a new perspective on everything. This new perspective will extend far beyond the immediate area of your wish. Situations in your life that once seemed acceptable may now feel out of place. You may also perceive the people in your life from a new point of view and respond to them differently.

To make space for your New Reality, you may even have to confront your nature on a physical or psychological basis. If you wish to be a successful public speaker, you will have to resolve your innate shyness. If your innate aggressiveness is pushing away relationships, you need to address and negotiate this trait.

Many people think that we can change ourselves only so much, that ultimately we cannot escape our hard-wired, DNA-encoded, biological destiny. And yet even here you can change yourself more than you realize. Stud-

ies have shown that by changing your behavior, you can actually change the physical chemistry of your brain. Even *pretending* to feel differently can begin this process.

Your biological nature may greatly affect your behavior, but your behavior can also greatly affect your physical nature.

◎

Although your New Reality requires that you make internal and external changes, you may not *want* to change. You unconsciously follow the deep grooves of habit. It is also quite likely that you've enjoyed some success with your current patterns (though not so much that you are satisfied with the way things are).

What's more, the human being is structured to maintain the status quo. Our body coordinates numerous complex physiological processes to maintain internal balance and stability. Similarly, our mental, emotional, and behavioral habits function to preserve the status quo.

Of course, change is often initiated by outside influences. These influences can be positive, in the case of a new love, or negative, in the case of an illness. Our tendency, however, is to return to the status quo.

◎

To make room for your New Reality, you will need to examine your life and see what changes are necessary. Consciousness is the first step in realizing our New Reality since we cannot change that which lies outside our awareness.

Just as you have begun to examine every aspect of your external life, you may also need to examine your internal life: your behavior patterns, your beliefs and expectations, and even your fears. You will be investigating old patterns and creating new, supportive ones.

Once you bring a wish into The Circle, your unconscious knows your intention. It now knows which parts of your beliefs, experiences, and life structures to present to you for examination. As you embody your New Reality, your subconscious is already beginning to reprogram and redirect your inner resources. Your subconscious will demand that you resolve any conflicts to your New Reality. You have put your unconscious on notice that anything inside of you—any pattern, situation, or way of being—that conflicts with your New Reality should be brought to consciousness for resolution.

You will become aware of parts of yourself that had remained buried—perhaps for decades. Some of these conflicts may be very old ideas or patterns from childhood that still guide your life. Once you enter The Circle, you alert your inner self to use your thoughts, your dreams, your memories, and your experiences to resolve these issues.

However, it requires far more energy to be ill or create a life out of balance than it does to be well. Your internal structure wants to be well and works toward health and balance whether or not you are helping.

There may be times, though, when your internal programs, whether physical, emotional, intellectual, or intuitive, do not contribute to your health and happiness. Indeed, your internal systems may sometimes even work against you. When this occurs, external support allows you to live in one part of yourselves while neglecting other parts for periods of time without sustaining damage. Your parents took up the slack in much of your everyday reality as children and young adults, allowing you to use that energy for growth and learning. In the same way, your friends, spouses, and children can support you in many ways, taking up the demands of your other systems while you focus on the one that requires your immediate attention.

In The Circle, you will feel the pressure and support toward the behaviors that create your New Reality. You may find yourself avoiding certain foods or desiring certain people, situations, or activities. You will find these things brought to you by "coincidence." When you make space in yourself and your life, enlightening ideas and circumstances will be attracted to you. The void becomes the well, and transformation takes place.

When you make space, you allow all of the parts of your being to work together. Resources, abilities, and talents that you have habitually ignored become available to you, sometimes for the first time. The Circle brings awareness to all of the parts of your being. This transformation creates a compelling force as you come into balance with yourself and your environment.

It is important that you strive to maintain internal as well as external balance. Each human being comprises numerous dynamic systems: intellectual, physical, emotional, spiritual, intuitive, creative, and many others. Each one of these systems, in turn, comprises numerous subsystems.

No individual's systems are each equally strong. Some are more developed, others less so. You have at least one system that is your strongest and one that is your most fragile. What's more, at any given time, one system may have far more demands on it than others. At any given time, you may have no major physical stresses, but you may have severe emotional or intellectual ones.

In times of stress, or when handling people or situations, you tend to turn to one particular system by reflex, your default system. Your default system is not necessarily your strongest. It is usually the one that you were genetically hard-wired to depend on, and the one you found most effective in dealing with your childhood environment. If you are wondering which system is your default, it is probably the one others characterize you by. If people had only one word to describe you, would it be "analytic" or "empathetic" or "aesthetic" or what?

You need to become aware of your default system because when you use one kind of energy at the expense of another, you deplete your being's ability to sustain itself. If you rely too much on your default system or any other, you do so at the expense of your overall health. If you respond intellectually to everything, then your emotional and other systems are paying the price.

Each of our systems needs nourishment as well as expression. You often keep balance by shifting from one system to another. In daily life, this means simply doing one thing each day to satisfy each part of you and each part of your life. Within and without, the life that you have created around you also needs to be brought into balance. In The Circle, different areas of your outer life—work, family, interests, and physical activities—all support one another toward the creation of your New Reality.

Think of ways to feed yourself. Contemplate a new idea. Take the stairs instead of the elevator. Talk to a dear friend. Take a moment to be grateful. Imagine yourself astral-projecting into the arms of a departed loved one. Return to a warm memory. Doodle. Write a poem. Hold hands. Get a massage. Listen to music. Nourish yourself by nourishing others.

When you make space, you free the parts of yourself and your life that have been stifled, engaging them in the act of transformation.

⊛ Ending the Battle Within dialogue to work w/ parts & how they are impacted by the New Reality

THE FIFTH
ELEMENT IS
MAKING SPACE

The gift of making space is
TRANSFORMATION

Take a long, deep breath and embody your New Reality. Become aware of your connection to The Circle.

Notice the feelings, memories, relationships, and concerns from your old reality that come to consciousness as you embody your New Reality more and more fully.

As you notice these pieces of your old reality, allow yourself to experience them in greater detail. Use all of your senses. Do you want to keep this old reality as it is? If not, what energy in it do you want to use to create a New Reality in your life right now? Make a conscious choice to use the energy in a new way, and use your breath and your connection to the energy of The Circle to let go of each piece of your old reality, one by one.

You may re-experience memories or forgotten feelings, or discover ones that you didn't know were there. The energy of The Circle will help you transform this energy to create your New Reality. Practice this every day, and the layers of your past will be liberated and become the materials of conscious creation. You may want to record your experiences in your Circle Workbook.

The Sixth Element
COHERENCE

If creating your dreams were as easy as selecting a wish and embodying it, why don't you have what you want today, right now?

When you analyze a lack of success in any aspect of your life, you tend to look outside yourself for the explanation. Yet often the answer is that you are getting in your own way.

We all work against ourselves some of the time. For many of us, this is true most of the time.

Listen to your own inner dialogue right now, in this moment. If you are like most people, you are worrying about, hoping for, afraid of, dreaming about many different things at once. You give yourselves many tasks, and often those tasks conflict with one another.

How many opposing desires do you live with in every moment? Your desire to be successful may be competing with your desire to be free from responsibilities. Your desire to fall in love may be competing with your desire to remain independent. Your desire to have a wonderful relationship may be competing with your desire to hold on to the bad relationship you are currently in. Your desire to raise a family may be competing with your desire to be recognized in your career.

It is natural to want to have your cake and eat it, too. And it is natural that most people remain frustrated in realizing their heart's desire.

Inner conflict is draining and disempowering. It depletes your resources without advancing you on any front. It's as if you were trying to open a door by pushing and pulling it at once. Rather than working toward one wish or the other, you are engaged in a battle with yourself. What's worse, your inner confusion attracts mixed and confusing experiences from others and your environment.

This kind of inner conflict is easier to see in others than in ourselves. One clue that it exists is a lack of progress toward our New Reality.

When you entered The Circle, your initial wish may have overshadowed other dormant, conflicting wishes. Yet sooner or later, these needs will reassert themselves. You cannot be productive if any two parts of you— values whether beliefs, or actions—are working at cross-purposes.

All parts of your inner being need to work together to create a balanced whole. When you are at one with your goals and desires, you are in a state of coherence. And when your intention and all your resources are in coherence, you can channel all of your human energy to achieve anything.

Hospice
for
Mom

Sometimes life compels us to concentrate for a period of time on one goal. At such moments, you are able to override any internal conflicting desires and call upon your resources to achieve that goal.

Recall those moments when you were totally focused on achieving something urgent—getting a report completed on time, getting a doctor in the middle of the night for a friend, coming up with the money to go on a vacation, finding a friend to help you through a crisis. Most of the time you were able to do it. Your attention and your energies and your resources were galvanized around a single goal.

The power released by pure, unopposed intention is awesome. Mothers have been known to lift vehicles weighing a ton off of their children. Under ordinary circumstances, they have trouble carrying the same child's weight in their arms. In the moment of crisis, they were able to marshal all their human resources toward a single goal, with incredible results.

The laser is a useful metaphor. Ordinary light is scattered and diffuse, with countless photons bumping into one another. As a result, the waves of these individual light particles interfere with and even cancel out one another. A laser works by aligning these individual waves. Now all the waves reinforce rather than work against one another. The result: Incredible power is channeled and released.

Your inner self will wage battle upon you if you sacrifice one part of your being for another. In fact, most of us live in this condition to some degree. When you realize the ways in which your desires can oppose each other, you can negotiate between them. The idea is to minimize this conflict by allowing it to produce solutions. You will be surprised by how ingenious you are at finding solutions within The Circle.

This is necessary work. To use the full power of The Circle, you need your own power to be as clear as possible. As you master the elements of human being, you will learn to negotiate between your New Reality and the rest of the parts that make up your life. When you find a way to resolve these opposing desires, your New Reality will be coherent with all of the parts of your life and being.

Ask yourself the question, "How does achieving my New Reality affect the other areas of my life, both positively and negatively?" The positive effects are usually ones that you are comfortable with. The negative effects are the ones you need to problem-solve and negotiate before your unconscious will allow your energy to be directed to your New Reality.

Suppose that your New Reality is, "My soul mate and I have a healthy new baby." At the same time, you are aware of another wish: "My work is dynamic and successful." Your goal now is to anticipate any conflict that may arise between these two wishes and resolve it in advance. These issues, and possibly other issues within them, need to be negotiated to help and not hinder each other in order for you to use your energy coherently. When you look at these issues, you may see that you need to do some intuitive brainstorming to come up with ways in which having a full work life would also allow you to have a family.

Sometimes you will find creative ways to have your cake and eat it, too. Otherwise, you will need to make compromises. Perhaps you can find a way to work at home when it comes time to raise your future child. Perhaps you realize that your career is more important to you at this point and that you can postpone having a child.

Notice that in the course of this process you may need to re-evaluate your original wish. You may enter The Circle with one wish and discover, as you move through the nine elements, that beneath that wish lies another, truer wish.

Be open-minded: This wish may be very different from what you expected. For example, you may have begun your journey in The Circle thinking that you wanted to change your career. When you realized that your lack of progress indicated inner conflict over that goal, you discovered that what you really wanted was to create a home and family.

Even here you could negotiate a creative compromise with these competing desires, perhaps changing your career to one that would support time and quality of life with your family.

Many great myths and stories in literature are about an individual's setting out in search of one goal—whether to win a gold medal or conquer a nation or build a business—then discovering that what he or she truly needed was something different. Your journey will probably be much the same.

The journey so far has helped you clarify your needs and brought you that much closer to finding your heart's true desire. Allow your wish to transform as you transform.

This transformation will happen as quickly and decisively as you resolve the issues and obstacles within yourself. The Circle will provide the insight and support you need to persevere and succeed.

You will discover the truest expression of your wish as you travel The Circle. The Circle will take you to the purity of your wish. In its purity lies its power.

THE SIXTH
ELEMENT IS
COHERENCE

The gift of coherence is
RIGHT ACTION

One way to help isolate and resolve the conflicting dynamics of your different wishes is to represent your various desires graphically. Once you have mastered the element of coherence, you can create right action—direct initiative uninhibited by conflicting goals and feelings.

Imagine your New Reality as the center of a circle. Imagine all of the other areas of your life that you value in small circles around it. You may want to draw this in your Circle Workbook.

Notice whether any of your Circles are in conflict with any others. You may want to write some solutions for the conflicts in order to create flow.

This can be an ongoing process. Your intuition, your intellect, your subconscious, your social and family interactions, and all of your resources will then be directed toward creating coherence and, from it, right action.

You may want to document the solutions that you receive. Remember, once you are conscious of something, it is a tool you can use for creation.

Mastery

The Seventh Element
OUTER ROADBLOCKS

As you embody your New Reality and create space for it, sooner or later you will encounter resistance. Sometimes, at the beginning of your journey within The Circle, it will feel as if everything is going wrong.

This is a sign you are making excellent progress! Before you can fully create your New Reality, you will undoubtedly experience one or more "roadblocks." Roadblocks are internal and external challenges we encounter when we introduce change into our lives. Left unaddressed, such challenges can stall or even prevent your New Reality from actualizing itself.

Because you are accelerating the process of wish-actualization by using The Circle, your roadblocks will come fast and hard. Good. The sooner you address them, the sooner you will conquer them.

Roadblocks are part of all change. Expect them. Welcome them. They show you which parts of yourself and your life block your growth and happiness. You decide to fall in love, and you are hit by your feelings of unattractiveness. Wham: You've been stopped dead in your tracks. You decide to create a company in your spare time, and your boss starts giving you extra work. Wham.

Hypnosis Private Practice

This is often the point at which people stop. They allow themselves to become overwhelmed by the obstacles, afraid of making wrong moves. Paralyzed.

In the past, you may have frozen in the face of obstacles. Perhaps you took them as signs that you couldn't or shouldn't have what you longed for.

When you embody your New Reality with the support of The Circle, you will be guided through the obstacles to your goal. In the process, you will lose your fear.

Conventional wisdom says that to get what you want, simply solve the problem, conquer the adversary. In The Circle, there are no adversaries, only energies that must be handled differently. The Circle allows you to experience a state of being in which the solution is lived. When you are within The Circle, obstacles present themselves as gifts to show you the way to a New Reality.

For every obstacle to your New Reality, you are also being presented with an opportunity. The things in you and in your life circumstances that block your New Reality are simply presenting themselves for resolution. When you free the energy held by these obstacles, your New Reality creates itself, fully, rapidly, and stunningly.

Remember that once you enter The Circle, obstacles to your New Reality become apparent along with synchronicities that herald its coming. The obstacles that you encounter work the same way as synchronicities. When you meet an obstacle, the Universe is inviting you to deal with it and create a change within yourself.

Once you understand what roadblocks are—and what they are not—you can move past them. Most of us were raised with the idea that what happens inside us and what happens outside us are two different things. What you are, however, determines much of what surrounds you. People in love attract love. People who can experience abundance attract abundance. If you look at the people and circumstances that surround you, they will draw an accurate picture of who you are at this time. In The Circle, you are transforming, and your life will be re-created with your changes.

If you hold fast to the energy of The Circle, you will be carried through the chaos of change. Realize that in the journey toward your New Reality, events rarely follow a predictable path. For now, simply recognize that once you enter The Circle, every time you hit a roadblock—whether within yourself or in the world—you have traveled that much closer to your goal.

Life is full of choices. You are being presented with the very situations around you—as well as the precise issues inside you—that must be resolved in order for your New Reality to be completely realized. In the past, you may have met these situations with fear or even anger. You may have reacted to things around you without ever resolving them. Now that you are within The Circle, you have the means, the energy, and the insight to make real change.

For example, you wish for a great-paying job in which your creativity is valued. All of a sudden, your fear around change is highlighted. This time, however, you confront that fear within the loving safety of The Circle. Now you talk about your fear with others, you even have dreams about it. You gather the tools to challenge it. You gradually remember where the fear originated and the experiences that reinforced it. Now, for the first time, you choose your wish over your fear. You transform the energy of fear into the energy of excitement. When the perfect job presents itself a month later, you are ready to accept it. You have, in fact, drawn it to you.

You tend to avoid creating miracles by living life through your fears. As you create your New Reality, doubts and fears will present themselves. The ability to wish is too often replaced by the capacity to dread. Dread undermines our commitment to creation. You find yourself swallowed by anger, envy, and grief over what is not, instead of committed to create what can be. Dread allows us to hold on to what we have and convinces us that reaching for our dreams is unsafe. As a result, we remain frozen in the familiar.

Take a moment to notice your habitual thoughts and reactions in reference to your wish before it became your New Reality. When you focus on love, do you feel you are most alone? When you focus on success, do you notice your failures? Acknowledge your fears, yet retain only the useful knowledge they impart. If your past efforts at success brought negative results, the elements of The Circle will help you understand why. These experiences will present themselves to you for resolution as you embody your success. Your conscious commitment to create your New Reality, as well as your mastery of the elements of The Circle, will heighten your awareness and create change.

Most of your emotional and intuitive energy is spent on repressing what you know in order to protect your soft underbelly. You feel too fragile to see that a relationship is not working out or that smoking will kill you. You use your energy to hide from reality. You blind and deaden yourself to avoid confronting difficult emotions or changes. Self-assertions reveal a lot about a person's fears. You pretend to be what you are not—which is invariably the opposite of what you fear yourself to be. One way to discover what people fear is to see where they put their focus and energy. Look at the perfectly put-together person and realize that person is probably afraid that he or she will fall apart.

In The Circle, you can use your fear. Notice the parts of you that cannot feel your New Reality. The voices of doubt and fear. The ideas, people, or situations that block the fulfillment of your New Reality. Notice the emotions and memories that come to your awareness, then exhale them into The Circle for resolution.

You see the facts that you have been hiding from, the ones you used to grieve, or fear, or despair. You also see the power you have to change them. When you are fully within the energy of The Circle, the truth of the past, the present, and the future actually becomes energy with which you can create your New Reality.

It takes courage to travel The Circle. It is sometimes a difficult journey as you encounter all of the barriers within you and around you.

The many secrets that you unconsciously keep from yourself will be unveiled. The flaws in your life and your surroundings will confront you. You must resolve to keep your intentionality, your will, focused on realizing your wish.

If you run away from your New Reality, you make your fear and denial and delusion more important than your being. The Circle rewards will by allowing it to be the fuel toward your goal. The energy of The Circle will support you. It will bring you what you need to prevail. For every difficulty that you meet head-on, a gift will be given; for everything taken away, there will be something even better replacing it.

For some of you the problem is deeper than fear: you have lost the ability to even imagine a better situation.

Many of us have visited a dark place called depression. In this region, your only wish is to be allowed to "give up." Your beliefs, your center, the things you hold dear all seem lost to you. If your core self is lost to you, for a time you are in a place of enforced isolation.

Yet from this emptiness, you can have a clear field for creation. Even from this place, you can recover your lost dreams. In fact, rock bottom is a solid foundation from which to build a New Reality.

Where I am now

Such moments are wake-up calls. The difference between those who fail and those who prevail is the latter's ability to marshal all of one's internal and external resources in the same direction toward a clear goal. Sometimes, a personal crisis forces such single-minded, laserlike focus of intention upon you at the moment when valuable resources—money, health, or even a clear sense of self—have been destroyed. You are torn between mourning what was lost and the pressing necessity to create something new, all in the absence of previously reliable resources.

Such times are often referred to as "the darkest hour." You may unconsciously create such apocalyptic moments to compel yourselves to make radically needed changes in your life.

Life can be perceived either as an inspiring challenge or a dispiriting struggle. When you perceive life as a struggle, you are continually confronted with situations that overwhelm you and bring up your inner confusion and helplessness. When you allow life to be a challenge, each area of ignorance brings an opportunity for mastery.

Its my choice

THE SEVENTH
ELEMENT IS
OUTER ROADBLOCKS

The gift of outer roadblocks is
INTUITION

When you have the courage to acknowledge and resolve outer roadblocks—to experience your present life and your past as they truly are—you free your intuition. Your intuition no longer has to help you "fool" yourself into staying stuck. Intuition will show you the problems, but it will also guide you to solutions.

Use your Circle Workbook to record your experiences of this exercise.

Enter The Circle.

Notice what you are perceiving and thinking in this moment.

Tell yourself that, on the count of three, all of your senses—thoughts, perceptions, even distractions like the phone ringing—will become sources of information that describe what helped you get to your New Reality and what you and your life are like when your New Reality is fully and completely in your life. If you are not perceiving anything, make things up. Pretending is a way to engage intuition, as it is the mind's "default" mechanism when you don't have the time or energy to be creative.

Count to three.

Everything you experience is now about your New Reality.

Write without pausing so that you don't have time to "think" or "reason." Ask your intuition questions. How far in the future is your New Reality completely realized? How is your life different? Who is in it? How have you changed? Who has helped you? What surprises you about your life in your New Reality?

You can do this exercise for another person by pretending that they are sitting in front of you at the point in the future when their New Reality is fully in their life. The person does not have to be present. You can communicate your experience to that person by phone or email.

If often helps if you do not know what the person's New Reality is (better yet, if you don't even know the person you are "reading") before you do the reading. The more you "know," the more the mind wants to reason with this information, interfering with the free flow of your intuition.

This is a wonderful sharing exercise to do in a group.

journal

The Eighth Element
INNER ROADBLOCKS

Y ou may already be living your New Reality. If so, you know how hard it was to release your old reality, no matter how unsatisfying it may have seemed at the time. If you are not living your New Reality, you may still be holding on to your old reality.

If you've ever had trouble leaving a bad relationship, or dead-end job, or changing even something as trivial as the channel on a television show, you know how difficult it can be to give things up. You can get some idea of the strength of your unconscious need when you continue to hold on to a situation, a thing, or a person when absolutely everything rational, reasonable, and conscious tells you to let go.

Children in tropical countries catch monkeys by placing a bright object at the bottom of a bottle attached to a rope. A curious monkey, attracted by the object, finds that it can just barely squeeze its hand into the bottle to grasp the object. The monkey discovers that it cannot pull its fist, clenched around the object of desire, back through the bottle opening. It is trapped because it refuses to drop the object and pull its hand free.

Your New Reality cannot enter your life until you are willing to let go of your old reality.

Having made your wish within The Circle, know that its realization has begun. The only thing that can stop the process at this point is . . . you.

Since wishing sets you in motion—indeed, sets the Universe in motion—it is vital that you become aware of your wishes. Be careful what you wish for, warned the ancient oracle, because you may get it. This is only partially true: we must be careful what we wish for because we will almost certainly get it.

If you have wished for things in the past but your most fervent prayers have gone unanswered and your most dedicated efforts seem to have gone unrewarded, the first place to explore is within. Your challenge is often not that so few of your wishes and prayers are going unanswered but that most of them are in fact being answered!

I have already discussed some of the reasons your wish, your New Reality, may have difficulty materializing. You may have conflicting desires, or you may need to make room in your life for your New Reality.

As you grow up, you are taught to focus all of your energy outward in times of adversity. The most difficult and intensely painful roadblocks, however, are not the obvious external barriers but rather the more subtle internal ones. These challenges are sometimes referred to as your "issues."

All of us know someone who wants desperately to be in love yet never finds a lasting relationship. Is this person intrinsically unlovable? No. This is someone who cannot fully embody the truth that being in love is both safe and desirable, or someone whose conscious actions are controlled by conflicting unconscious goals.

In the sixth element, coherence, you confronted conflicting conscious wishes. Now you enter the realm of unconscious wishes, and the unconscious is a messy place indeed.

In your unconscious, all of your experiences and memories and your interpretations of them—even if you were three years old when you made the interpretation—are woven together to create a picture of yourself, of others, and of the world and your place in it. Your unconscious mind accepts this picture and makes it the basis for the guiding principles in your life.

Let's say that a youngster's parents divorce and his mother gets a job. From the infant's perspective, this becomes internalized as an absolute equation: career success equals emotional separation. Though you have long since forgotten many of the formative incidents from your childhood, your unconscious mind still accepts these lessons as "truths."

Our problems as adults can often be traced to faulty assumptions formed long ago. You want career success but you also want emotional intimacy. In your unconscious mind, these are mutually exclusive wishes. Unless you consciously strive to question the "facts" upon which your unconscious is operating, you will continue to live your life at their mercy.

Your current needs are not those of a five- or ten-year-old, even if that child was you. Indeed, your unconscious wishes are very often the direct opposite of what you consciously want in your life right now.

Tacky success

In the past, you were following a life path largely designed by your unconscious as a result of childhood experiences that you have long since forgotten. But now that you are an adult, you need to consciously re-design your path to cope with adult experiences.

A wish long ago forgotten may be destroying your life now. The manifestation of unconscious wishes often hits our lives like sudden explosions, with pieces of shrapnel destroying our conscious creations.

This examination process is rarely comfortable since there is always a reason that you have kept what you wanted from entering your life. Perhaps being ill allowed you to avoid the problems in your marriage. Perhaps being unsuccessful kept you feeling safe and insulated. Perhaps getting into relationships with the wrong people allowed you to ignore your own feelings of inadequacy.

We arrange many of life's great tragedies for ourselves. We tend to look outside ourselves for our failures.

If you have had difficulty attracting success into your life in any area, there is a good possibility that you are avoiding that success for some reason. This avoidance becomes your hidden agenda.

Hidden agendas are ulterior motives that you have within yourself—goals or values or needs that you are largely unaware of, yet which often conflict with your conscious goals.

You may have a hidden agenda to avoid being successful. Perhaps it's because you feel you don't deserve success, or because your unconscious senses that any business success may threaten the stability of your family life.

After all, if you really believed that you could create your New Reality—and that you deserved it—your wish would already be in your life. One reason you express your wish in the present tense, as though you have already achieved it, is to draw out these issues ahead of time. The sooner you recognize your issues, the sooner you can work them out and clear the way for your wish.

Negative Wishing

You are always wishing, though you may not always hear your wishes. The process of unconscious wishing is so subtle that you must beware even the questions you ask yourself. Consider the following ones: Why am I sick? Why don't I have enough money? Why am I alone?

Though framed as questions, these are actually wishes, and negative ones at that: I wish I weren't sick, I wish I weren't so poor, I wish I weren't alone. When you focus on "sick," "poor," "alone," that is what your attention and energy are creating. When you say, "I feel miserable," the myriad reasons that you are miserable are highlighted in your life. Your attention finds misery everywhere and increases that state of being.

You may be trapped living in the terrain of forgotten wishes. You may have wished you were the prettiest girl in second grade. You may have wished that your parents didn't fight so much at the dinner table. You may have wished that you could make your high school basketball team or be accepted at your first-choice college. Or you may have wished that everyone would just leave you alone.

You may have made those wishes ten, twenty, thirty years ago or more. You may still be creating these wishes unconsciously in the present, and today those long-forgotten wishes may be tearing apart your life. Your childhood wish to be left alone may have been answered—so you finally are alone, and lonely.

Choice can neither be forced nor artificial. You cannot bully yourself into putting your energy into a wish just because you think you should. The Circle will not work for a false goal, because you cannot work with all of the parts of yourself toward that goal. A part of you will always be resisting.

The subconscious knows when you are fooling or forcing yourself, and it will fight you if a real desire or need is being ignored. You will not allow yourself to achieve in a false direction without interference from the conflicting parts of yourself. It is exhausting to fight with oneself. The internal battle consumes energy, while keeping you stuck in your present situation. Conflict drains your life force and depresses every part of you. But when you make a wish that you really want, one from the deepest parts of your being, your journey becomes a fluid and joyful expression of your self.

If any part of your being rejects your wish, you must negotiate within yourself.

The spine is an appropriate metaphor here. If you attempt something out of alignment with your spine, with the beliefs that make it worth being you and life worth living, then you cannot complete that action effectively.

When you bring a wish into The Circle, these conflicts become illuminated, and you are pointed in the direction of resolution.

When you become aware of how a part of you can oppose your own desire, you can negotiate between them. Using your inner resources and intuition can help you find a way, for example, to be successful and still feel comfortable that you are not neglecting your family. Your unconscious would not allow you to become successful at the expense of your family. If you want love but your childhood taught you that you were unworthy of affection, you can now consciously sort through those messages. You have all of your inner resources at your disposal to create agreement.

The catch is that you are not the master of your own conscious mind; your unconscious is always maneuvering as well. The great difficulty with confronting your unconscious, of course, is that it's unconscious. After all, you can never become completely aware of your unconscious motivations no matter how hard or long you search. You can, however, work with your unconscious toward greater awareness and self-mastery.

*Become aware of theaw/
Active Imagination + the Other
mindset*

How can you overcome the power of your unconscious wishes? The answer is to put energy behind your intentionality.

Remember the power of your hungers. In The Circle, old conflicts and patterns are transformed through the power of focus and intentionality. The energy of the Universe is directed by the intensity of your wish. The more passionate you make your conscious wishes, the more they will prevail over any conflicting unconscious wishes.

If you dedicate yourself to a course of action consciously, chances are that you will succeed. Even if you are not now able to transcend your hidden agendas, you can at least become more aware of their impact in your life.

You now know the dangers of unconscious wishing. Without awareness, you can spend lifetimes digging your foundations until they become your graves. To gain the full power of The Circle and direct the powers of the Universe, you must learn to take conscious control of this process.

Your goal, then, is awareness. Once you are conscious of something—whether a behavior or a value or a hidden agenda—you are more able to make the choice to move beyond it. With awareness, you can create anything in an instant.

The gift of inner roadblocks is

HEALING

Take a long, deep breath and enter The Circle. You may want to return to the meditation on page 24 to reconnect with the energy of The Circle.

Breathe fully and deeply, filling every atom of your being with energy.

Know that with every breath you take, you will continue to fill every atom of your being with energy.

When you feel so full of energy that you can hold no more, place your hands in front of you, palms facing each other a foot or so apart.

As you breathe, allow the extra energy to flow between your two palms.

Play with the energy between your palms. Make it warmer, cooler, quicker, happier. Again breathe fully and deeply, pulling more energy into your being and allowing the extra energy to flow between your hands.

If you now put your hands on a person, you are doing a healing.

If you imagine a difficult situation between your hands and allow the energy to flow into it, you are doing a healing.

If you put your hands over a photo of someone in need, you are doing a healing.

If you hold hands with another, you are doing a healing.

If you place your hands on yourself, you are doing a healing.

The Ninth Element
CONTACT

Until now, it may have seemed as if you were traveling The Circle by yourself. But you are not alone. When you need courage or other resources, strengthen your contact with The Circle by inviting others in.

Now that you are fully within The Circle and embodying your New Reality, you have begun to encounter others with whom to co-create your New Reality. You now realize that the people or situations brought into your life are there because you have invited them to create your New Reality.

The Circle itself is an experience in community and integrity. When you consciously enter The Circle, you enter a pattern of energy contained by everything in the Universe, the pattern of creation. This energy is the same whether you are creating inner health or a world empire. When you enter The Circle, you join every other being, energy, and event at the point of oneness. From this point, you affect all, and all affects you.

As you experience The Circle more and more frequently, others who embody this energy will join you in your life. Your community will have integrity, and you will bring integrity to it. You will find that the lovers, helpers, friends, and others who enter your life have an innate understanding and willingness to help you create your New Reality. In turn, you will be motivated to help others achieve their New Realities.

When all of your inner resources are working together, you have integrity. When you are working with integrity in the world around you, you have community. In The Circle, your community extends even to people you have never met.

The Circle has no beginning and no end. You are energetically connected to everything around you. People and events are working with your intention. Every person and every event is programmed to help you create your New Reality with you as you create their reality with them.

Your ability to connect your energy, your heart, your presence, your intuition, and your healing to other beings is perhaps your greatest resource. Once you master the element of contact, you can heal others as you are being healed.

Every day you meet, you greet, you work with, and you love others. In The Circle, you experience these connections in their greatest depths. You connect to one another through your individuality. You offer your differences and your uniqueness as gifts to one another.

A baby is at first aware only of its own needs. Then the awareness extends to its connection to its mother. As the infant grows, its awareness extends to include first its family, then others, then society at large, and beyond.

The more broadly your awareness extends, the more power your being has. Once you become aware that you, as a single being, can affect people and events thousands of miles or many years away, your energy consciously begins to touch and influence an ever-broadening range. You begin to realize the full power of human being.

The Universe sustains you as you sustain the Universe and one another. You will find yourself meeting other people who have chosen to be fully within The Circle.

The larger your Circle grows, the more powerfully you can create. The energy of two people focusing together is far greater than the simple sum of two.

This is so dramatically true that soldiers marching across a bridge are instructed to march out of step with one another. Armies adopted this practice when it was discovered that a group of individuals in step with one another can cause sufficient vibrations to make a bridge literally come crashing down.

Use this energy positively by expanding your Circle.

The more you connect with others, the greater your opportunity to complete the energy of The Circle. Think of a computer that runs on electricity. If you don't plug it in and complete the circuit, it can't do anything. If a sequence is missing in its programming, it can't run properly.

When you connect with others, you "complete the circuit." The unique gifts and experiences of each individual complement what you may be missing.

When you are at one with the energy of The Circle, then the clarity of your intuition, the strength of your healing, and the mere presence of your physical being support the positive creation of others. When you make contact with them, your focus is how you can help them create their own New Reality. Sometimes you offer healing, other times intuitive insight, an embrace, or a hand with their everyday needs.

You will enter the lives of others whom you can assist without draining or diminishing yourself. If you have extra time, money, or talents, you will be presented with opportunities to share what you can with others.

When you pass someone in need on the street, you energetically bring this person into The Circle for healing. When you touch another, whether it is a momentary exchange, a brush of a shoulder, or a warm embrace, you will send healing to them as they send healing to you. You will embody the best reality possible for everyone around you.

Although money is the medium of exchange in today's world, any exchange of time, energy, or other resources plugs us into the energy of connectedness. You can connect your energy to that of others in countless ways.

Trade readings with your best friend each morning. Donate money to your favorite causes or institutions. Offer resources to a friend who is struggling. Give precious things that you no longer use to someone who needs them. Listen to someone who is lonely. Help your employees move ahead. Forgive when you can.

When you see a need, ask if you can fill it. When you have a need, ask that it be satisfied.

⊚

The more you travel The Circle, the more people will enter your life wishing to give you what you need. You will attract people and situations that have what you need. You will learn to accept that which is offered without feeling debt, just as you give without expecting gratitude.

⊚

In The Circle, giving frees up the space for new things to come into your life and being. Receiving what you need is your opportunity to do this for another.

You will begin asking yourself what you need that day and what you have to give. Every meeting will be a sacred exchange of energy. Abundance will spill into your life and from your life, just as waters flow without effort from rain to stream to river.

We all need different things at different times. We all have a surplus of something. Give what you have. Ask for what you need. This reciprocity within The Circle creates abundance for all.

As you heal, you in turn are healed.

Just as you formalized and empowered the process of embodying with rituals, you can empower your Circle by creating a physical circle of like-minded others. A group's energy can be united around a prayer, an idea, a belief, a meal. Once you unite the energy of a group, you make contact with the energy of The Circle. You may want to collect some friends and do The Circle together, or have a Circle moment with your family each day. Together, we each become increasingly powerful agents of one another's New Reality.

You can create beautiful rituals with others. A spring renewal, a celebration of healing, a group healing for a friend going through a hard time, or a gifting ceremony for the birth of a baby or a project. Ask each person to bring a little ritual of his or her own for everyone to do.

When you include those around you in your rituals, you strengthen your community as well as your New Reality. In The Circle, the most powerful gifts are received while you yourself are in the act of giving. When you create rituals that include others—a party, a meal, raising resources for a cause you believe in—you attract energy to create your New Reality while co-creating a New Reality for others.

You will find that when you help another, you also help yourself. There is a story in the Old Testament about Moses who, radiating, lays his hands on Joshua, who also begins to radiate; yet in giving light to Joshua, Moses

Very Impt.!!

doesn't radiate any less brilliantly himself. From this comes the saying that a candle does not lose its flame by giving light to another candle. When you share your light in The Circle, you live in a brighter world. This light extends all around you and travels around The Circle infinitely.

The Circle is entered with hands open, to give what you have to give and to receive what you need.

There are unique ways of giving within a group Circle. You do not give what strains you. If you are short on time, do not offer to give away what little you have. If you are short on money, conserve it. Maybe someone in your Circle is a great organizer and can help you improve your efficiency. Maybe you have enough money, and you could pay this person well for helping you.

As you work together, you do so from the vantage point of the questions, "What more can I give to this person?" and, "What more can we offer those around us together?" At the same time, you are each focused on getting your own needs met by each other and by the world around you.

When each person embodies his or her New Reality in The Circle—sharing the energy of healing, intuition, intent, and humanity—the participants create a strength far greater than that of one individual.

Now you will begin to experience the full power of human being in The Circle. You will see that the whole Universe now supports your New Reality. You are now The Circle.

The gift of contact is
UNITY

According to the physical laws of wave mechanics, the intensity of waves that are in phase with one another is the square of the sum of the waves. When we embody the energy of The Circle together, the energy for creation increases exponentially in its magnitude.

When you enter The Circle, you are always with a group of people working with you and for you energetically. When you create a physical Circle, with others present, both collective energy and the resources you can provide are astounding. Whether among friends, family members, or "strangers," the Circle can immediately create harmony, healing, and community when practiced in a group. A group Circle can be done with one other person or a thousand other people. The important element is Unity.

Here is how to form your group Circle:

1. Do something to give the group a common energy or pulse. You can do a taped or spoken guided meditation (such as The Circle meditation), say tongue twisters together, sing a song that everyone knows, or do anything else that allows people to come together.

2. Have each person silently choose a wish or New Reality to achieve.

3. Have all the participants embody their New Reality with all of their senses and notice any resistance, images, intuitions, or feelings that arise as they fill their bodies with breath and the embodiment of their New Reality. Ask them to breathe, and to feel themselves and The Circle as one, allowing the energy of The Circle to help them release what they need to let go of, attract what they need to draw to them, and transform any energy of illness or dysfunction into an energy that supports their New Reality.

4. Do a group sharing or paired exercise. You can get these exercises from my series of Practical Intuition books or other books on intuition, self-therapy, or healing. You will eventually want to create your own. You can ask others in The Circle if they want to share an exercise with the group.

5. Have the group come back together as a Circle and do a healing meditation where each person embodies his or her own New Reality, embodies one another's New Reality, and as a group sends this energy of their New Reality out to every other atom of the Universe, so that the Circle of creation that has been formed includes everything in the Universe.

You may want to include a moment where each person experiences the full energy of the group. I often ask people to go around The Circle and state their New Reality (or a symbol that represents it, if they want to keep their New Reality private). As each person does this, the others in the group direct healing energy toward the person and his or her New Reality.

You can also ask people to state what they have to offer—what they can easily offer—and to ask for what they need. This can be personal help, support, cash, advice, legal help, anything at all.

The Circle is a ritual in itself. You may want to add a ritual to The Circle. In my books as well as books devoted to ritual, there are exercises that can be converted to rituals. The best rituals are ones that you create yourself.

If you are doing a Circle on a specific subject, you can integrate old, familiar rituals into your Circle. You may want to do a baptism for new beginnings or a funeral for endings, where each person says a brief eulogy to what he or she no longer needs; you may want to put a candle for each person in the center of The Circle, to be blessed by the energy and lit in his or her home. You can include other people in your Circle for healing by writing their names on a piece of paper and putting it in the center of The Circle. You may want to pick a time each day where each of you puts your energy consciously into The Circle that you have created.

Be creative. Trust your own ideas.

You can adapt The Circle for any environment. In a business setting, you can create a Circle by telling a joke, eating together, or doing anything that gives the group a common energy. If you identify the focus of The Circle, such as coming up with a new marketing plan or getting a project out on time, you focus the group on a New Reality. You can ask the members of the group what they need from or have to offer their coworkers to help this happen. You can have participants embody the result without seeming "weird" by simply asking, "What does the end result look like to you?" This focuses the group on a present, positive reality and enlists its resources in creating it.

Feel free to frame The Circle in the language that will be acceptable to your group. A group of doctors, investors, mystics, or therapists will each have their own language. Use your observation skills and intuition to know what that language is. If your group is mixed, use your intuition to find the common language.

The closing is as important as the opening. Once again, do something that creates a common energy or pulse in the group. It could be a round of handshakes, a cup of coffee, or an expression such as "It's happening" or "Done!"

Often, family rituals provide their own realities, such as the evening meal, or simply getting everyone up and going in the morning. You might want to ask your family members what they would like these rituals to feel like. If you have no family rituals, create some, even if it is just sharing the paper in the morning. These rituals provide the unity that allows a family to create a common reality. If there is no common goal, focusing on the reality you would like to create for your family will guide the energy. Remember, when someone's energy is focused with integrity, it is stronger than the many scattered energies around it.

More than a decade ago, an energetic healing circle was created. At 9 P.M. EST, people all over the country center and allow themselves to become part of a community of people sending and receiving healing.

No matter what your religious background, prayer circles—or, for that matter, any group wishing you well—are energy circles. You may want to try expressing your New Reality on the many internet prayer and healing lines or at your local church or synagogue. You can also post your New Reality on www.practicalintuition.com.

Your Reality and your being are most precious and powerful when shared. I embody your New Reality in my Circle as you embody my New Reality in yours.

In The Circle we are one.

EPILOGUE

When you consciously enter this place we call The Circle, you can create and transform anything—yourself as well as the world around you. In The Circle, what you perceive, what you conceive, and what you create are one. You are one with the infinite energy and possibility of creation.

There are no breaks, pauses, stops, or endings. When you put down the book, you remain in the journey. When you pick it up again, you travel further on your path.

Each person, each event, each moment, each possibility that has been, or ever will be, exists here and now in The Circle.

Nothing is lost. Nothing begins, and nothing ends. Everything simply is.

Experience presents itself in a framework we call space and time, with a past, present, and future. But your life is not a series of points along a time line. There is a place where all of the points connect—The Circle.

You are at one with the past and with the future. Every person and every event that have ever existed or will exist are here now with you in your Circle of energy. You are a part of everything. In The Circle, your past, present, and future are all taking place now, in this moment.

The Circle, like your unconscious, does not distinguish among a "past," a "present," and a "future." It is all happening now.

One of the things you will learn from being in The Circle is to overcome the limitations imposed by our conventional notions of past, present, and future.

Albert Einstein showed that the timing of events depends on the vantage point of the person observing those events. Time does not exist within The Circle. The past and future exist together—right now—in the present.

I realize that for many people this is a radical concept, but the more time you spend within The Circle, the more natural this perspective will become for you.

⊚

Paradoxically, the future exists right now. So does the past. Recognizing this is the key to changing the future as well as the past.

Your original perception of an experience, the moment itself, will always exist in all of its transformations. Your experience of a moment simply is where you direct your focus of attention, your consciousness. You can change a moment in the past as easily as you can change a moment in the future. When you change this moment, the one you are experiencing now, you change eternity.

⊚

Everything is perceived, created, dissolved, and transformed in the present. You can change the past, the present, and the future by creating in this moment.

A Circle has no beginning and no end. You can enter The Circle at any point in your life. Once in The Circle, you can revisit and revise all the points in your life, whether past, present, or future.

You can change your reality by changing any part of this formula. You can change the future by creating a goal and directing your resources toward it. And you can change the present by sending out a different vibration and being selective about what you receive. You can even change the experience of the past.

It is usually the energy and patterns of the past that form barriers to creating the New Reality in our lives. Now that you are within The Circle, you may notice that memories are visiting you. Some of these memories may be painful. Within The Circle, you can re-experience, revise, and heal them.

Allowing yourself to experience the reality of the "past" in this moment is far easier than allowing your experience to shift perspective from the "past" to the "future."

If there is an energy created by something you did or didn't do, something said or unsaid, change it now. Place your attention on that moment and experience the energy of that moment as it should have been. Continue to do this until it feels right.

When you embody your New Reality, you are doing this in the future. You are changing what you perceive in the future, and as you do that, the past re-creates itself to support you. Hold someone you've lost. Go back and visit them in a shared moment in the past, or bring that person to your consciousness now. Allow yourself to feel his or her presence and the energy that the two of you will always share together.

By re-experiencing and re-interpreting your past, you can change the energy and vibrations that evolved from it.

No person, no thought, and no event remains unaffected by the energy of The Circle. Every person, every event, every moment, every possibility that has been or ever will be exists now in The Circle.

As you read these words, know that I am in The Circle with you, and you are in The Circle with me.

The Circle
Workbook

"In The Circle all the gifts of human being are mine.
I am enough, right now, to create anything I dream."

OUR WORKBOOK

Your ability to manifest your dreams is directly related to your ability to consciously connect with all your inner resources and tap into the infinite resources of the Universe. You are about to learn that you have far more inner resources than you ever realized.
—LAURA DAY

When you do The Circle, you use your powerful human gifts the way they were meant to be used: to create your goals and dreams. It is the system by which you take an idea, a wish, a need, and you create it in the physical world. Knowing that there is an efficient, time-honored system for creating what you want should compel you to make this a daily practice.

I live The Circle every day—except when I forget. I now realize that my times of forgetting are often preceded by "busy" times or "involved in a drama" times or even joyful times that conveniently take me away from both the power and the grief in remembering. I don't even know I have forgotten until life begins to get tangled and the clear and gentle flow of my days turns turbulent. When that happens, I use this Workbook to carry me through and deepen my ability to use The Circle. It helps me to create what I want in the physical world as well as to purify my desires, heart, and goals so that I continue to become someone I can love and respect. When I look back on what I've written in the pages of my Workbook a day, a month, a year later, I can behold an intuitive history of my growth as well as a clear and concise map for my future, complete with obstacles, tools, choices, and wonderful happenings I would have perhaps otherwise missed. The most powerful oracle you have is your own intuition—trained, documented, and followed daily. These Circle Workbook pages will bring it out of that wonderful messy place called the human mind and into your able hands.

So much of life is lived in the head. The human mind is a wonderful place, but to create change, things need to be built in the physical world.

What I love the most about The Circle is its ability to gently peel the husk from the perfect life that exists for all of us. With ever-increasing depth and speed, as you use The Circle, you find, within you and therefore in the world around you, everything you need for life, health, love, creativity, abundance, and joy.

Following The Circle Workbook pages will keep you on your path, away from old patterns that have stopped you from opening the door to the life you want. I have experienced this in myself and with the many Circles I have been part of over the last ten years. You can create anything. You can change anything. You can be anything if you walk, even the tiniest steps, around The Circle.

This is how I do it: by making a commitment each day with my Circle Workbook pages and then letting the energy of The Circle do the rest. I do them "in the fashion of" *The Circle* book. What does this mean? I do not always start with the first pages of the Workbook. There will be times when I need to start with, say, Making Space, because that is what I find I need most. I don't even always do a full page. I commit to quality, not quantity. Sometimes a wish must be approached from the inside of my being to then become reality in the world. There are times when I cannot deal with the limitations within me until I change something in my world first. Each part of *The Circle* finds your power through a different process. It doesn't matter where you start.

The first section of the Workbook includes Daily Exercises. Come here to figure out how to get to where you intend to go. Often, after time passes, when you refer back to these broad stroke pages you will find very poignant, fine, and accurate details that you missed the first time around.

The second section of the Workbook has Weekly Exercises, where you can work on an intention in greater depth. When you find yourself reaching a roadblock in this section, move on to the Anytime Exercises, where you will be able to tackle your obstacles even more deeply.

The Anytime Exercises are really your pages of truth and teaching. They will reveal to you your own inner wisdom as well as give you a process that you can do with others, in a group, or when leading your own Circles. Come to these exercises when you are feeling lost while working on one of the elements or when something is not working out. The Anytime Exercises provide the cure for these moments.

Finally, you will find the Affirmations of the Elements section. These affirmations will offer you guidance and will enhance the experience of The Circle in your life. You can make a ritual out of this section and experience one of the affirmations at any time of the day. Of course, you can create your own affirmations, as well.

You'll notice that I've taken some quotations from earlier in the book and placed them before related exercises in the Workbook. I have also included page references in case you want to revisit that particular section.

There will be days when it takes ten Workbook exercises—or even many more—for you to turn a situation around. Other times, a single page may be enough.

I try to carry a copy of *The Circle* with me at all times. I ask everyone involved to sign it so that it holds the energy of the new communities I become part of every day. I do *all* nine elements of The Circle technique briefly at the gym (headphones on) as I always seem to skip, in my memory, the element that in the moment I most need. Every time I do an element of The Circle it is a different experience for me, depending on my wish, my mood, what parts of my self, body, challenges, or community I am addressing on that day. When I start a new wish, I often get a new workbook and ask a group of friends to commit to being in The Circle with me for that particular wish, sharing healing, intuition, resources, and energy to co-create a New Reality for each of us, together.

There is no "right way" to do these exercises, but doing them every day will keep you moving toward your wish even when other things are dragging you under.

The Circle belongs to you. Own it, use it, teach it, and add your own story to its wisdom.

The Circle
Daily Exercises

◎

"To enter The Circle you need only to make a wish."

TODAY'S ELEMENT IS . . .

INTENTIONALITY

I embrace my awareness of my heart's deepest desire.

I do not judge its worthiness.

I accept my desire as a perfect part of me and myself as a perfect part of the
Universe.

TODAY'S GIFT IS . . .

CONSCIOUS CREATION

I make a wish and I write it down as if it had already happened.

I wish in the present and in the positive.

My one deepest wish is happening now.

It is my New Reality.

I, _HAVE 10 MILLION DOLLARS_ , (write your wish in the circle below)

10 MILLION
DOLLARS (US)
BEFORE THE AGE OF 40.

FOR SURE!!!

TODAY'S ELEMENT IS . . .

EMBODIMENT

I experience my wish come true, my New Reality with all my senses. I experience it in every moment. When feelings, thoughts, and judgments interfere with my experience, I take a deep breath and let them go or I share them with people whose intuition, judgment, intellect, and counsel I trust.

Write below your experience today of your New Reality—in the present tense. Include feelings, inner observations of your New World, the new people, places, opportunities, and experiences that you are sensing around you.

_____

_____

_____

_____

_____

_____

_____

_____

_____

_____

_____

_____

TODAY'S GIFT IS . . .

AWARENESS

My experience of each day brings to me a greater awareness of all that is around me and within me to create my New Reality in my life now. I, _____, affirm my commitment to my New Reality.

Below write the new awareness and intuition (about the present, past, and the future) that today has brought you.

_____

_____

_____

_____

_____

_____

_____

_____

_____

_____

_____

_____

_____

TODAY'S ELEMENT IS . . .

RITUAL

I am becoming aware of patterns in my life that do not serve me in my New Reality. Each day I pick one pattern and I replace it with a thought or action that I consciously choose that supports my New Reality. Everything I do is conscious and empowering.

Write a habit that you need to change (and why) and the ritual that you are replacing the habit with. Be simple and inventive!

_____

_____

_____

_____

_____

_____

_____

_____

_____

_____

_____

_____

_____

_____

TODAY'S GIFT IS . . .

SACREDNESS

I, _____, acknowledge myself, my actions, and my life as sacred and powerful. I allow every word, thought, and deed to empower me to create change in my life and my world. Even the simplest act becomes a ritual, conscious and empowering, to bring me closer to my New Reality.

Write below what releasing your old pattern and replacing it with your intentional ritual will bring into your life.

_____

_____

_____

_____

_____

_____

_____

_____

_____

_____

_____

_____

_____

TODAY'S ELEMENT IS . . .

SYNCHRONICITY

I notice the meaningful, helpful coincidences that occur daily in my life—every person, every event, co-creates my New Reality with me. I am aware of my oneness with the Universe around me.

Write the coincidences that are happening for you now so that your subconscious can be encouraged to allow more of them into your life.

_____

_____

_____

_____

_____

_____

_____

_____

_____

_____

_____

_____

_____

_____

_____

_____

TODAY'S GIFT IS . . .

EFFECTIVENESS

My every thought, action, encounter, challenge, and blessing brings me closer to my New Reality. I, _____, am co-creating my New Reality with the help of the world around me.

Write below the way that synchronicities you have experienced have improved your life and made it work more easily and effectively.

_____

_____

_____

_____

_____

_____

_____

_____

_____

_____

_____

_____

_____

_____

TODAY'S ELEMENT IS . . .

M A K I N G   S P A C E

    I choose to release any obstacles, thoughts, interactions, habits, and beliefs that do not support my New Reality.

    Below write the things, feelings, relationships, and beliefs that you are consciously letting go of today and how you are choosing to go about doing it.

_____

_____

_____

_____

_____

_____

_____

_____

_____

_____

_____

_____

_____

TODAY'S GIFT IS . . .

TRANSFORMATION

I, _____, use my energy and the energy of the Universe around me in a new way. When I experience a block, I use the energy of The Circle to transform it into my New Reality.

Now that you have freed up the energy held in the situations that you are letting go of, write below how you are going to use that energy—now yours to direct, to have, achieve, or become.

_____

_____

_____

_____

_____

_____

_____

_____

_____

_____

_____

_____

_____

_____

TODAY'S ELEMENT IS . . .

COHERENCE

All the elements of my life work together to support my New Reality. When I become aware of a conflict between one part of my life and my New Reality, I use everything available to me to resolve it consciously. I am empowered to find solutions.

Below list the different conflicted areas of your life, which could use improved communication and resolution.

_____

_____

_____

_____

_____

_____

_____

_____

_____

_____

_____

_____

_____

TODAY'S GIFT IS . . .

RIGHT ACTION

I, _____, come up with the perfect solutions to fit the different areas of my life together in a seamless and empowering way. My thoughts, actions, and deeds heal my life as they bring me closer to my New Reality.

Negotiate between the areas of your life that need more agreement and below write the solutions as they come to you through your negotiation. The negotiating can take place inside your head or on paper or even in a conversation with someone!

_____

_____

_____

_____

_____

_____

_____

_____

_____

_____

_____

_____

_____

TODAY'S ELEMENT IS . . .

OUTER ROADBLOCKS

I allow myself to be aware of the situations in my life that need healing and change. I am unafraid to see clearly as I know the power of The Circle and my own human being will support me in creating positive change.

Write below the situations that you feel need to be "faced" in order for you to achieve your New Reality.

_____

_____

_____

_____

_____

_____

_____

_____

_____

_____

_____

_____

_____

TODAY'S GIFT IS . . .

INTUITION

I, _____, am open to receiving clarity and infor-
mation from the world around me. My courage to see clearly is based on the knowledge that I am infinity powerful to create change. I am supported by the whole Universe
in creating my New Reality. I share my intuition with those who ask for my guidance.

Write below some loving, reassuring guidance for yourself. Allow it to flow onto
the page without your thinking about it!

_____

_____

_____

_____

_____

_____

_____

_____

_____

_____

_____

_____

TODAY'S ELEMENT IS . . .

INNER ROADBLOCKS

I have a lifetime of wishes within me. Some of them even I am unaware of. I choose to become aware of my hidden agendas and to give energy only to the wishes that are current, nurturing, and empowering. I choose my New Reality.

Write below some old wishes, dramas, or beliefs that you are ready to put to rest now.

_____

_____

_____

_____

_____

_____

_____

_____

_____

_____

_____

_____

TODAY'S GIFT IS . . .

HEALING

I, _____, am healed, physically, emotionally, spiritually, and in the reality of my life. Healing is my birthright. It is a part of me. I choose to use all of my energy toward the path of wholeness and creating the New Reality I have chosen.

Write below the things in your life and in your body that you are choosing to heal/change now. As you write them on the page, know that the simple act of "putting them down" begins the process of healing.

_____

_____

_____

_____

_____

_____

_____

_____

_____

_____

TODAY'S ELEMENT IS . . .

CONTACT

Even when I feel most alone, I am in contact with all of the energy and beings of the Universe. Alone is a feeling that comes from within me and not from the Reality of human being. When I make contact with another human being, my being and energy are multiplied exponentially.

Write below all of the caring around you: the connections you have, no matter how small or brief, that may be directing kindness toward you now. Describe how you are directing your kindness and sense of connection outward to the world.

TODAY'S GIFT IS . . .

U N I T Y

No great thing was ever created by one man alone. I, _____, am part of the Unity of energy in the Universe. My New Reality is being co-created with me and for me by every energy in the Universe. I am co-creating the New Reality of others in The Circle. I am part of a community of energy, of love, of creation. I am in The Circle and I am never alone. I am home.

Write below what help you request from the Universe and the people in it right now. Include what you have to offer. Commit to asking for these things (both through direct requests and prayer) and to offering what you would like to give to others as well.

_____

_____

_____

_____

_____

_____

_____

_____

_____

_____

_____

The Circle
Weekly Exercises

MY NEW REALITY

Week One

The first element is I N T E N T I O N A L I T Y

The gift of intentionality is

C O N S C I O U S   C R E A T I O N

The Circle is an energetic state of being that allows you to connect with yourself, with one another, and with the transformative powers of the Universe. In The Circle, what you perceive, what you conceive, and what you create are one—and you are at one with the infinite energy and possibility of creation (page 2).

You may have many desires, so it may not be easy to decide on just one. For now, though, you must choose just one wish to create as you master the nine elements of The Circle (page 11).

Begin this week by noticing the one thing/change you want more than anything else, right now.

Know that there is an alchemy to wishing. In the past you may have been disappointed by wishes that have not come true. When you wish in The Circle, you wish in the language that the Universe understands and will respond to (pages 13–15).

Make this wish in the positive and in the present tense (pages 14–15) as if it had already happened. Put the wish in the circle below (page 16). Feel free to also draw the wish or to create a symbol that represents it.

May 19, 2011

I won the lottery worth over 30 million dollars now!!.
We are free from financial worries!!
It is great!
I give my 2wk notice to MRMC!

Week Two

The second element is E M B O D I M E N T

The gift of embodiment is A W A R E N E S S

Now that you have made your wish, it is crucial that you experience it as if it has already occurred. To embody your wish is to embrace it today, right now, even though it may not have completely manifested itself to you (page 17).

At first it may be difficult to embody your New Reality (your wish come true). There may be a place within you that cannot fully feel, see, or experience your wish. Learning to embody fully takes time and practice. The more fully you can embody your wish in the present, the more quickly it becomes real in fact (page 19). Once you embody your wish, it is your New Reality.

Practice experiencing your New Reality by doing the meditation beginning on page 24.

Allow yourself to experience all the many ways your wish could come true (pages 18–20).

Write below, outside of the circle, some of the thoughts, memories, and feelings that get in the way of you experiencing your New Reality fully. Once you become conscious of an obstacle, it will change from an impediment into a tool.

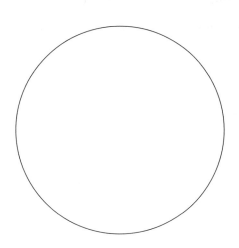

When you fully embody your New Reality, you reprogram the messages you are sending out and the world meets you with new opportunities.

Week Three

The third element is R I T U A L

The gift of ritual is S A C R E D N E S S

The third element, Ritual, furthers this process by replacing many of your unconscious habits that have no connection to your current wish with conscious rituals that reflect it. Rituals are an external equivalent of embodiment. Rituals imprint your wish in your environment, everyday actions, and outer life.

Pick a few habits that do not support your New Reality and create rituals to replace them. Do these rituals whenever you would otherwise act out your old habit.

Do rituals with your friends and family, even if you just eat a meal of celebration or bless each other during breakfast to energize and co-create one another's New Reality.

The best rituals are created by you, for you. Try the ritual guide on page 36. Write below the habits you are replacing and the rituals that will replace them.

_____

_____

_____

_____

_____

_____

_____

_____

Rituals are distinguished from habits, the soulless reflexes that allow us to so easily sleepwalk through our lives. Rituals are important because we inject them with meaning. The difference between rituals and habits is the difference between the sacred and the mundane. Rituals give you the power to change your world.

Week Four

The fourth element is S Y N C H R O N I C I T Y

The gift of synchronicity is E F F E C T I V E N E S S

By making a wish and embodying it within The Circle, you have sent a clear signal to the Universe. The process of change within The Circle has begun. Your wish is already coming true. You don't need to "do" anything. All the energy of the Universe is now focused on creating your New Reality with you.

You may want to re-experience the meditation on page 24.

Notice how you have created a pulse, a rhythm in your life that embodies the pattern of your New Reality. Find new ways to embody this rhythm.

Notice the meaningful coincidences, both pleasant and difficult ones, that have been happening to you and around you since you entered The Circle, and write a few of them below so that your subconscious can realize that you are empowered to create what you choose.

_____

_____

_____

_____

_____

_____

_____

_____

_____

_____

_____

_____

_____

_____

_____

_____

_____

_____

_____

_____

_____

So, now that you have wished within The Circle, be aware that the pieces of your New Reality are already being presented to you. The usefulness of these synchronicities may not become apparent until days or weeks or even months later. Nonetheless, never lose sight that once you have entered The Circle, all these events will conspire to move in the direction of your New Reality.

Week Five

The fifth element is M A K I N G S P A C E

The gift of making space is T R A N S F O R M A T I O N

Your New Reality needs space. When you focus on creating something new, the Universe requires that you grow, and space is a pre-condition for growth. The Universe needs space to bring everything you have asked for into your life. The changes you will need to make may be difficult. You may notice that you need to let go of certain situations and people in your life.

As you embody your New Reality this week notice what people, situations, and beliefs you are holding on to that may no longer serve you. You don't need to "amputate" these things from your life drastically. Instead, write some of them below, and as you write them down feel that you are letting them go.

_____

_____

_____

_____

_____

Notice what you make space for when you let go. Notice how your feelings, thoughts, and energy directs itself in new ways. Take some notes on the new ways that you use this energy now. Notice how this changes your inner being. You may re-experience memories or forgotten feelings, or discover ones that you didn't know were there. The energy of The Circle will help you transform this energy to create your New Reality. You may want to experience the exercise on page 56.

_____

_____

_____

_____

_____

_____

_____

_____

_____

_____

_____

_____

_____

_____

_____

_____

Week Six

The sixth element is C O H E R E N C E

The gift of coherence is R I G H T   A C T I O N

How many opposing desires do you live with in every moment? Your desire to be successful may be competing with your desire to be free from responsibilities. It is natural to want to have our cake and eat it, too. And it is natural that most people remain frustrated when trying to realize their heart's desire. Inner conflict is draining and disempowering; it depletes your resources without advancing you on any front. It's as if you were trying to open a door by pushing and pulling it at once.

If you had your New Reality right now, which other parts of your life/self would have to make adjustments? Take a few moments to write down a few of those other life areas. You may want to do the exercise on page 63.

_____

_____

_____

_____

_____

How can you negotiate between your New Reality and the other areas of your life or being that are important to you? Who can help you by their actions or ideas? Can your intuition give you solutions to any conflicts that arise? Notice the solutions that come to you for creating coherence between your New Reality and the rest of the important goals and structures in your life. Write some of these solutions below.

_____

_____

_____

_____

_____

_____

_____

_____

_____

_____

_____

_____

Your inner self will wage battle upon you if you sacrifice one part of your being for another. When you realize the ways in which your desires can oppose each other, you can negotiate between them. The idea is to minimize this conflict by producing solutions. You will be surprised by how ingenious you are at finding solutions within The Circle. You can engage healing, intuition, prayer, a therapist, friends, the wealth of your world, in this process.

Week Seven

The seventh element is

OUTER ROADBLOCKS

The gift of outer roadblocks is INTUITION

When you have the courage to acknowledge and resolve outer roadblocks, to experience your present life and your past as they truly are, you free your intuition. Your intuition no longer has to help you "fool" yourself into staying stuck. Intuition will show you the problems, but it will also provide you with solutions.

When you embody your New Reality, which "realities," situations, or relationships do you find bring up the most fear, anxiety, or anger for you? Write these down, and use your intellect, intuition, discussions with friends and/or counselors to deal with your awareness of these roadblocks.

_____

_____

_____

_____

_____

_____

_____

_____

Remind yourself of other times in your life when your external situation was difficult, when you were in a real pinch and you found a resolution. Remember the positive ways in which the crisis changed you and your life. Practice believing in your own power to create positive change in your life.

Practice the intuition exercise on pages 74–75 and allow your intuition to guide you to your New Reality. You can also practice this exercise with a friend, your family, or any other kind of group.

Rock bottom is a solid foundation from which to build a New Reality. Such moments are wake-up calls. I often refer to these times as "the darkest hour." You can unconsciously create such apocalyptic moments to compel yourself to make radically needed changes in your life.

Week Eight

The eighth element is

INNER ROADBLOCKS

The gift of inner roadblocks is H E A L I N G

In your unconscious, all of your experiences and memories and your interpretations of them—even if you were three years old when you made the interpretation—are woven together to create a picture of yourself, of others, and of the world and your place in it. Your unconscious mind accepts this picture as true and makes it the basis for the guiding principles of your life. You get some idea of the strength of your unconscious when you continue to hold on to a situation, a thing, or a person when absolutely everything rational, reasonable, and conscious tells you to let go.

Embody your New Reality and allow yourself to notice where in your body, memory, and emotions you feel discomfort, insecurity, or a disharmony with your New Reality. Allow those areas to become clearer and more detailed for you. They don't necessarily have to "fit" or "make sense." Allow yourself to experience them, and write them down below.

_____

_____

_____

_____

_____

_____

You may notice that as you experience your inner roadblocks, insights, solutions, and healing occurs. Write them down below as they occur to you. You have the answers and the ability to heal. Do the healing exercise on page 85. You can do this alone or with others.

Unless you consciously strive to question the "facts" upon which your unconscious is operating, you will continue to live your life at their mercy. How can you overcome the power of your unconscious wishes? The answer is to focus your energy on your intentionality. In The Circle old conflicts and patterns are transformed through the power of your focus and intentionality. The energy of the Universe is directed by the intensity of your wish. If you dedicate yourself to a course of action consciously, chances are that you will succeed.

Week Nine

The ninth element is C O N T A C T

The gift of contact is U N I T Y

The more broadly your awareness extends, the more power your being has. Once you become aware that you, as a single being, can affect people and events thousands of miles or many years away, your energy consciously begins to touch and influence an ever-broadening range. You begin to realize the full power of human being.

Offer something that you have to give to at least one other person and ask at least one other person for something you need. In The Circle we all have something to give and something that we need. Abundance is created through sharing. Write below a few things you have to share and a few things that you need others to share with you.

_____

_____

_____

_____

_____

_____

_____

_____

_____

_____

_____

_____

_____

_____

_____

_____

Do healing on yourself and someone else daily. Remember that as you embody your New Reality and increase your Circle of contact, you create your New Reality.

Create a Circle with others. Practice Unity with the exercise beginning on page 94.

You will find that when you help another, you also help yourself. There is a story in the Old Testament about Moses who, radiating, lays his hands on Joshua, who also begins to radiate; yet in giving light to Joshua, Moses doesn't radiate any less brilliantly himself. From this comes the saying that a candle does not lose its flame by giving light to another candle. When you share your light in The Circle, you shine and you live in a brighter world. This light extends all around you and travels around The Circle infinitely. Now you will begin to experience the full power of human being in The Circle. You will see that the whole Universe now supports your New Reality.

The Circle
Anytime Exercises

○

MY NEW REALITY

"The Circle is entered with hands open, to give what you have to give and to receive what you need."

M Y   N E W   R E A L I T Y   .   .   .

In The Circle, what you perceive, what you conceive, and what you create are one. Make one wish in the positive and in the present tense (as if it has already happened) and write it below (pages 2–16).

MY NEW REALITY TALE . . .

"Let's say a person's New Reality is to earn her living through her art. Her reality tale might go something like this:

I gave some of my pottery, my favorite hobby, away as gifts. A woman at a friend's dinner party saw a piece that I had made. As it turns out, this person ran the design department for a chain of stores. She asked for my phone number and called me for an interview to design a line of pottery for her stores. Within a few months, I received other offers. I felt secure enough to quit my job at the accounting firm. This step had the added benefit of leaving me the time and energy to go to the gym regularly. After a short time, I was in great shape and more relaxed than ever. At the gym, I met a wonderful man on the treadmill next to mine. We were married later that year and moved into a great apartment that had a studio space so that I could work at home" (pages 19–20).

Write your New Reality tale below . . . be as specific as possible!

_____

_____

_____

_____

_____

_____

_____

_____

_____

MY NEW REALITY TALE (CONTINUED)

MY NEW REALITY

COLLAGE . . .

Collect photos, magazine clippings, etc., that support your New Reality. Create your New Reality collage by pasting those things below.

RITUALS THAT EMBODY MY
NEW REALITY . . .

Sometimes doubts arise and we have difficulty embodying our New Reality in our minds. At such times rituals keep our New Reality moving forward.

You can create a ritual around anything, from the way you get up in the morning to the way you greet strangers, to the way you prepare your food. Set an extra place at the dinner table for the partner you expect to enter your life. Light candles when you bathe, and allow the water to "dissolve" your extra weight as the candles "melt" it (page 35).

Create several of your own rituals and write them below . . . remember to perform them regularly!

1. _____

_____

_____

_____

_____

_____

_____

2. _____

_____

_____

_____

_____

_____

_____

3. _____

_____

_____

_____

_____

_____

_____

4. _____

_____

_____

_____

_____

_____

5. _____

_____

_____

_____

_____

_____

_____

SYNCHRONOUS EVENTS THAT HAVE OCCURRED IN RESPONSE TO MY NEW REALITY . . .

Notice how the events around you begin to respond to the pulse of your New Reality.

Record the synchronicities that you encounter: the obstacles that you become aware of and the people and events that come into your life "out of the blue" to help you create your New Reality. Effectiveness is the result when you work with the element of synchronicity" (page 45).

_____

_____

_____

_____

_____

_____

_____

_____

_____

_____

_____

M A K I N G   S P A C E   F O R   M Y
N E W   R E A L I T Y . . .

Take a long, deep breath and embody your New Reality. Become aware of your connection to The Circle. Notice the feelings, memories, relationships, and concerns from your old reality that come to consciousness as you embody your New Reality more and more fully. As you notice these pieces of your old reality, allow yourself to experience them in greater detail. Use all your senses. Do you want to keep this old reality as it is? If not, what do you choose to release? What do you NOW create with this energy in your New Reality? Make a conscious choice to use the energy in a new way, and use your breath and your connection to the energy of The Circle to let go of each piece of your old reality, one by one.

Practice this every day, and the layers of your past will be liberated and become the materials of conscious creation (page 56). Record your experiences below.

_____

_____

_____

_____

_____

_____

_____

_____

_____

SOLUTIONS TO CONFLICTS IN ORDER TO MAKE MY NEW REALITY COHERENT . . .

If creating your dreams were as easy as selecting a wish and embodying it, why don't you have what you want today, right now? When you analyze a lack of success in any aspect of your life, you tend to look outside yourself for the explanation. Yet, often the answer is that you are getting in your own way (page 57).

When you are at one with your goals and desires, you are in a state of coherence. All of your energy is powerfully focused and directed toward a single, unambivalent goal. When your intention and all your resources are in coherence, you can achieve anything (page 58).

As you find a way to resolve opposing desires, your New Reality will be coherent with all of the parts of your life and being (page 60).

Imagine your New Reality as the center of a circle. Imagine all the other areas of your life that you value in small circles around it. Notice whether any of your Circles are in conflict with any others. You may want to write some insights about the conflicts in order to create flow. This can be an ongoing process. Your intuition, your intellect, your subconscious, your social and family interactions, and all your resources will then be directed toward creating coherence and, from it, right action. Remember, once you are conscious of something, it is a tool you will use for creation (page 63).

Allow yourself to become aware of your conflicting wishes and write them below. In so doing, you will crystallize the pure, powerful core of your wish and empower its creation.

OUTER ROADBLOCKS

As you embody your New Reality and create space for it, sooner or later you will encounter resistance. Sometimes at the beginning of your journey within The Circle, it will feel as if everything is going wrong. This is a sign you are making excellent progress! Before you can fully create your New Reality, you will undoubtedly experience one or more "roadblocks." Roadblocks are internal and external challenges we encounter when we introduce change in our lives. Left unaddressed, such challenges can stall or even prevent your New Reality from actualizing itself.

Because you are accelerating the process of wish-actualization by using The Circle, your roadblocks will come fast and hard. Good. The sooner you address them, the sooner you will conquer them (page 67).

When you have the courage to acknowledge and resolve outer roadblocks—to experience your present life and your past as they truly are—you free your intuition. Your intuition no longer has to help you "fool" yourself into staying stuck. Intuition will show you the problems, but it will also guide you to the solutions (page 74).

Complete the exercise on pages 74–75 and record your intuitions below.

_____

_____

_____

_____

_____

_____

_____

I N N E R   R O A D B L O C K S

Your New Reality cannot enter your life until you are willing to let go of your old reality. Having made your wish within The Circle, know that its realization has begun. The only thing that can stop the process at this point is . . . you.

You may have wished that everyone would just leave you alone. You may have made this wish ten, twenty, thirty years ago or more. You may still be creating this wish unconsciously in the present, and today that long-forgotten wish may be tearing apart your life. Your childhood wish to be left alone may have been answered—so you finally are alone and lonely.

Choice can neither be forced nor artificial. You cannot bully yourself into putting your energy into a wish just because you think you should. The Circle will not work for a false goal, because you cannot work with all the parts of yourself toward that goal. A part of you will always be resisting.

The subconscious knows when you are fooling or forcing yourself, and it will fight you if a real desire or need is being ignored. But when you make a wish that you really want, one from the deepest parts of your being, your journey becomes a fluid and joyful expression of your self.

If any part of your being rejects your wish, you must negotiate within yourself.

The energy of the Universe is directed by the intensity of your wish. The more passionate you make your conscious wishes, the more they will prevail over any conflicting unconscious wishes. Your goal, then, is awareness. With awareness, you can create anything in an instant (pages 77–84).

Complete the exercise on page 85. When finished, you may want to record any resulting thoughts or feelings below.

CONTACT . . .

Until now, it may have seemed as if you were traveling The Circle by yourself. But you are not alone. When you need courage or other resources, strengthen your contact with The Circle by inviting others in.

Your ability to connect your energy, your heart, your presence, your intuition, and your healing to other beings is perhaps your greatest resource. Once you master the element of contact, you can heal others as you are being healed.

Every day you meet, greet, you work with, and you love others. In The Circle, you experience these connections in their greatest depths. You connect with others through your individuality. You offer your differences and your uniqueness as gifts to others.

The more you connect with others, the greater your opportunity to complete the energy of The Circle. Think of a computer that runs on electricity. If you don't plug it in and complete the circuit, it cannot do anything. If a sequence is missing in its programming, it cannot run properly. When you connect with others, you "complete the circuit." The unique gifts and experiences of each individual complement what you may be missing.

You will enter the lives of others whom you can assist without draining or diminishing yourself. If you have extra time, money, or talents, you will be presented with opportunities to share what you can with others.

When you pass someone in need on the street, you energetically bring this person into The Circle for healing. When you touch another, whether it is a momentary exchange, a brush of a shoulder, or a warm embrace, you will send healing to them as they send healing to you. You will embody the best reality possible for everyone around you.

You can connect your energy to that of others in countless ways:

1. Trade readings with your best friend each morning.
2. Donate money to your favorite causes or institutions.
3. Offer resources to a friend who is struggling.
4. Give precious things that you no longer use to someone who needs them.
5. Listen to someone who is lonely.
6. Help your employees move ahead.
7. Forgive when you can.

When you see a need, ask if you can fill it. When you have a need, ask that it be satisfied (pages 87–92).

You see . . .

Who You Are Makes a Difference

AFFIRMATIONS
OF THE ELEMENTS

THESE AFFIRMATIONS WILL HELP YOU
ENHANCE YOUR EXPERIENCE WITH THE CIRCLE

INTENTIONALITY

I choose this goal _____ (mention your goal or wish) and in choosing it, all of my attention and strength from every area of my life is shared with the parts of me that need to come together to create this goal in the world. It is my Reality from now on; it is the place my thoughts go, where my senses live. I choose from this new sense of purpose. I employ courage to stay with my choice as my old reality tries to get in the way. In fact, the fuel from the struggle between where I was and where I choose to be gives passion and heat to my chosen direction. I am learning a New Reality and teaching it to the world around me. I create the world I live in and I am creating it now, with every breath I take, in every moment of the night and day, when I am awake and asleep. My New Reality is being created within me and around me because my intentionality is that powerful. It is the natural way of life for everything to follow the strongest force. I have chosen this New Reality and the power in choosing this one direction leads me and all people and events around me in its creation.

_____

_____

_____

EMBODIMENT

I choose to communicate powerfully and clearly to the world around me as well as to the various parts of myself. I engage all experience in the creation of intentional reality. I become, embody, all my senses as my senses send a powerful directive to the world around me. Just as I experience and respond to the energy of others, they respond to me, especially when I embody a clear message: my New Reality, alive and evolving within me and therefore in the world around me. When I embody, the people and experiences even the challenges I need come into my life. Because I, too, am growing my Reality, my life, even how it feels to be me, changes with every breath I take. As long as I embody or become my New Reality, everything, everyone changes within me and around me to co-create my New Reality with me. I no longer *have to*—I simply have to be, to fully experience my New Reality.

_____

_____

_____

RITUAL

I choose a single ritual to replace a pattern that holds me fixed in a reality I choose to leave. I may—instead of berating myself—bless each bite of food to give me a body I love or an elixir of attraction so welcoming that I no longer eat alone. In fact, I may use prayer as my exercise. Instead of engaging in behavior that used to harm me, I may first put my hands in prayer, as a signal that what I do next will bring me closer to my New Reality. My patterns, habits, reactions, compulsions no longer bother me once I recognize them and simply put a ritual in their place. When I have the courage to replace an old pattern with a new ritual, I take the mundane and I create the divine. Instead of stumbling through a maze of patterns and habits, I empower my sacred intention to create something blessed in my life. Each conscious choice, no matter how tiny it may be, gives me more of the power to change reality and easily change myself.

_____

_____

_____

SYNCHRONICITY

Even reading this passage now is a synchronicity. Unlike a coincidence, synchronicity is a guide to where I am going, what I will meet, and how safely or easily I will arrive at my destination. As I move through my day, all that I encounter—people, situations, places, things—exist to shift and guide me to my chosen reality. Nothing is a coincidence, luck, or chance. All has been divinely engendered by my proper use of the power we all share in creating reality. Even what at first seems difficult is useful in directing, consolidating, and redirecting my many gifts to achieve a world that fits my dreams. As I continue my awareness and practice of The Circle, these synchronicities will compose the major part of my experience. I will shift and all will move around me. If I encounter a setback, an obstacle, I will immediately, effortlessly know how to readjust and redirect to manifest what I had originally requested. Everything I intend is now a powerful and effective source of change. With every breath I take this process continues, becoming an internal shift guided by my intuition and guiding me to the creation of my New Reality.

_____

_____

_____

MAKING SPACE

As my life fills with the people and things I really want and need, all that I have outgrown makes space for my New Reality. Transitions occur seamlessly with my full and sure participation as I allow space to be made and space to be filled by the profound act of intentional transformation. Within The Circle, every changing moment loosens the binding attachment of the past, allowing me to bring forward only that which affirms my right to be whole, loved, successful, and joyful in the world. Old sacrifices, made to survive, are no longer needed as I reclaim the power of my original being. As I feel the grief of loss, I also feel the joy of recognition and transformation and the clear, sure knowledge that what I will create will be exactly what I need to be complete. This change is happening now.

_____

_____

_____

COHERENCE

If I focus all my powerful gifts on my New Reality, responding each day to the opportunities that I am presented with, I allow my growing New Reality to touch all of the areas of my life that are important to me. It is strengthening them, enlightening them, evolving them. As I negotiate the challenges between each of the areas of my life, I create new potential for pleasure and power. This negotiation and strengthening continues even when I am not consciously aware that it is going on. I experience this shift through the fluid working of my life and relationships. I step into each moment well prepared and am able to experience and manage the various areas of my life with ease and joy while creating more abundance than I could ever have imagined. All this and more is happening now whether or not I feel secure in the changes and even when my feelings are not at peace. I know that I am actively negotiating well on my own behalf to reach my New Reality.

_____

_____

_____

OUTER ROADBLOCKS

Looking around my life I experience things in a state of change. I have the insight and the strength to see things as they really are so that I can use my many tools to create the change I need. I have courage born of ability and self-knowledge. Situations that I used to hide from to spare myself pain or change I am now able to face with clarity, peace, and empowerment. Addressing my life in a realistic way enables me to confront even long-standing issues with pleasure and momentum. I am my own best example of humanity as I tell no lies to myself and I allow none to be told to me. It is in the pure, fresh air of my life that the fire of my desires burn away all outdated impediments to my New Reality. I can sit with the truth and have the patience to act when I am ready for the very best outcome. What I learn from honestly facing the outer roadblocks in my life empowers me to choose my best interest in the present and in the future. The skills I learn from my outer roadblocks are truly mine and are gifts to me that last forever. As I gain the courage to see my life with clarity, I open my life to possibilities so wonderful that they make each day a blessing.

_____

_____

_____

INNER ROADBLOCKS

Inside of me live all the many people I have been. Each of me, at every age, had wishes and rules of my own. In the past I have lived following patterns, rules, and goals that are stored in the treasure chest of my subconscious. I now, with the surety of today, allow myself to question patterns and beliefs that no longer serve me. I consciously choose what is appropriate and true for me now, thereby allowing new, wonderful experiences and people into my life. As each old pattern becomes conscious for investigation, I acknowledge my skill and love in guarding my precious self as I find more inclusive ways to keep myself safe while allowing a new and desired reality into my life. I transform with ease as my life mirrors my own inner wisdom and flexibility by attracting all that I desire into my field. I am blessed by life's abundance and by my own ability to choose appropriately for myself in a new and inspired way.

COMMUNITY

I am part of a field of energy, which includes everyone and everything. When I make a shift the world moves with me. I am never alone and at the same time I am a defined individual within the energy that we all share. This awareness allows me to move in my world in a way that chooses the people and situations that create my desired goals with me. I am the teacher and the student as I co-create my New Reality with a willing and loving world. I am useful and all around me is useful to me. The unity of all being supports me, guides me, and heals me as I play a part in this unity with conscious intention. I am home.

Look for Laura Day's new hardcover book
How to Rule the World from Your Couch
in Fall 2009